UNDERSTANDING ANIMALS

Others books by Lars Svendsen also published by Reaktion Books:

Fashion

A Philosophy of Boredom

A Philosophy of Fear

A Philosophy of Freedom

A Philosophy of Loneliness

UNDERSTANDING ANIMALS

Philosophy for Dog and Cat Lovers

Lars Svendsen

Translated from Norwegian
by Matt Bagguley

REAKTION BOOKS

To Kari Händler Svendsen (1944–2017),
who taught me how to understand animals.

Published by Reaktion Books Ltd
Unit 32, Waterside
44–48 Wharf Road
London N1 7UX, UK
www.reaktionbooks.co.uk

This edition first published 2019
Copyright © Lars Fr. H. Svendsen. First published by Kagge, 2018.
Published in agreement with Oslo Literary Agency.

Matt Bagguley asserts his moral right to be identified
as the translator of the work.

This translation has been published with the financial support
of NORLA

Printed and bound in Malta
by Gutenberg Press Ltd

A catalogue record for this book is available from the British Library

ISBN 978 1 78914 159 7

Contents

Introduction

Anyone who has ever had a pet has wondered how the animal perceives the world, or how it feels to be in the world of a dog or cat, for example. No dog or cat has ever written an autobiography telling us anything about it. When I see a moose, fox or hare on a woodland road, I wonder how they perceive me. When we see nature programmes on TV where an eagle glides, a killer whale swims or an octopus walks on the seabed, we try to imagine what it's like to be in the consciousness of these animals. American biologist Stephen Jay Gould writes:

> Give me one minute – just one minute – inside the skin of this creature. Hook me for just sixty seconds to the perceptual and conceptual apparatus of this other being – and then I will know what natural historians have sought through the ages.[1]

It is, as Gould somewhat mournfully points out, impossible. We can do nothing more than work indirectly, study these creatures from the outside and always remain in wonderment at what actually goes on in their consciousnesses, and how it is to be present in the world of one creature or another.

This is not primarily a book about animals, but about humans. Of course we humans are also animals, but we are animals with a range of characteristics that no other animals have. This book, therefore, is about what possibilities there are for us humans to understand animals that are not humans. The book is a defence of the amateur's view of the animal, and I would argue that an amateur's relationship with animals is just as valid and insightful as the scientific view. Having said that, the amateur might learn a lot from the scientific findings. For example, if you want to understand an animal, it helps to have some knowledge of the animal's evolutionary history, which will provide explanations that facilitate understanding. This book will therefore contain a lot of scientific material. In my opinion, however, the sciences can also learn something from the amateur's view. The amateur is, as the word quite literally means, one who loves – and that loving view in itself can reveal something that the distanced one cannot grasp. Martin Heidegger objects to the saying that love makes us blind, and emphasizes rather that love allows us to see things we cannot see when we do not love.[2]

If my approach in this book can be linked to a particular philosophical tradition, it is the hermeneutic tradition. This might seem strange to anyone familiar with this tradition, since it has typically dismissed animals from the domain of understanding, claiming that animals are something that can only be explained, not understood. One goal of this book is therefore to draw animals into hermeneutics, or the theory of interpretation; something from which they have traditionally been excluded.

In studies of animal mental life, chimpanzees and pigeons are over-represented. Cats and dogs show up far less often, but there is also an exhaustive amount of literature on them. In this book, there will be a lot about cats and dogs because they are the animals most of us are closest to in our daily lives. Chimpanzees are far closer to us genetically and evolutionarily, but very few of us have a chimpanzee at home, something which both chimpanzees and humans should be happy about. The proportion of cat and dog researchers who have all their fingers intact is far higher than that of chimpanzee researchers. Cats and dogs are more at home in our lives than chimpanzees are. This book will make good use of the observations I have made of my own cats and dogs – particularly Luna the dog and the cats Lasse and Geir, who will feature regularly in the text – for the simple reason that you learn a lot about an animal by living with it for many years. Of course, many other animal species will be included, and since the book is called *Understanding Animals*, that understanding should be put to the test; so I have chosen to give a little extra attention to the giant Pacific octopus, an animal with an advanced consciousness. However, since it has less in common with us than most other animals, it presents a real challenge. Understanding an octopus is like understanding a visitor from another planet.

The motto of the SETI programme, which searches for intelligent life on other planets, is a question: 'Are we alone?' Meaning more precisely: 'Are human beings alone, as intelligent life, in the universe?' The answer to the question is evidently a resounding no! Admittedly, I am a little agnostic on the question of whether there is intelligent life, or any kind of life, on other planets. On our planet, Earth, there is plenty of intelligent life, in addition to the *Homo sapiens sapiens* species. While writing these lines, I am sitting in the family cabin, where I have retreated for a few weeks to write undisturbed. However, I am not completely undisturbed because I have no doubt at all that there are *two* conscious beings here, or two subjects if you like: my dog and myself. We go for a walk now and then, and chat a little. It's not like in the movie *Cast Away* (2000), where the protagonist, stranded on a desert island, draws a face on a volleyball, talks to it and calls it Wilson. The volleyball evidently has no consciousness – but I have no doubt at all that my dog, Luna, does. That she is an example of *intelligent life* is obvious, but I ask myself, can I *understand* this variant of intelligent life that is quite different to my own? Can I understand Luna? Can I understand what it's like to be her?

This is a *philosophical* analysis of our relationship with animals. The purpose is to use philosophical perspectives which the individual reader may include in their own reflection of our relationship with animals. Ludwig Wittgenstein wrote: 'Work on philosophy ... is really more a work on oneself. On one's own conception. On how one sees things. (And what one expects of them.)'[3] Self-reflection like this cannot be done for you. You have to do it yourself. Rather than giving clear answers, I hope that I can, above all, contribute to the reader seeing something that would otherwise have been overlooked; and think thoughts that might have remained unthought.

ONE

Wittgenstein's Lion
and Kafka's Ape

'If a lion could talk, we could not understand him.'[1] Ludwig
Wittgenstein's assertion strikes us as strange. Most of us think
that if an animal could speak, we would understand it. The lion
would then be able to tell us what it's like to be a lion, instead
of us having to deduce it from the lion's behaviour. What does
Wittgenstein really mean by this remark? What kind of language did he imagine this lion would speak? German? English?
'Lionish'? If he means to say that the lion speaks, but that it
speaks 'Lionish', a language we do not understand, then it goes
without saying that we would not understand it. On the other
hand, he could also have said: 'If a Maasai can speak, you cannot
understand him.' That is obvious, since I'm no expert in Maasai.
But Wittgenstein seems to be trying to say something more
than simply the tautological claim that one cannot understand
languages one does not understand.

More precisely, one can imagine that he wants to highlight
a chasm between the human's world and the animal's – a chasm
so deep that understanding would be impossible, even if, for
argument's sake, we assumed that the animal could speak a language that consisted of the same words and the same grammar as

English, for example. Of course, I have never met an animal that speaks, if speaking means speaking like humans do, for the simple reason that no animal other than humans speaks like humans do. On the other hand, I have never interacted with an animal that did not speak. I have seen animals that do not speak, but these have been ones I have never been actively involved with. When I have encountered animals that I have tried to understand, they have spoken without exception, but of course it is me who has spoken for them. When I have tried to understand what is happening in the animal's consciousness, I have been unable to avoid articulating this understanding linguistically, as if it were the animal itself that spoke. I too am speaking to the animals. Not because I suffer from any illusion that the animal understands my sentences, as other people understand them, but because that is the way I communicate, and it seems as if I manage to communicate *something* with these sentences, albeit just a slightly undefined mood or a primitive command.

If Wittgenstein, in his wording, intends to draw a fundamental distinction between humans and animals, we must ask what the basis for that distinction is, and when it emerged. What if I say: 'If a Neanderthal could speak, we would not understand him'? Most people would think that a Neanderthal who speaks would be a being we could understand. Most likely, we would categorize this being as 'a human being'. However, the Neanderthals were quite different to us modern humans and, among other things, they had larger brains. They certainly had better eyesight than us, as larger parts of their brains were devoted to this, while their social intelligence was probably nothing to brag about compared to ours. When did man become a human being? At what point in human evolutionary history were we in a position to categorically pass the judgement: 'If X could talk, we would not understand him'?

When we look at the geometric signs made by our ancestors during the last ice age, we have to admit that we understand very few, if any, of them.[2] The amazing drawings of bulls and other animals are one thing; we believe we have an understanding of them because we can see what they depict. But we have to admit that we cannot say we understand much about the meaning of these images, since we know so little about the role they played in the lives of these people. The 32 documented geometric signs are quite another; we're at an even greater loss because we have no idea what they depict. We at once see them as expressions of meaning, but *what* meaning? We know a little bit about the people who made these signs – how they were dressed, hunted, used musical instruments and buried their dead – but we know nothing about the behaviour associated with the use of the geometric signs. If we could go on a journey in a time machine, we like to think we would be able to understand them, little by little, by interacting with them and getting to know their way of life. That way we could also see what role these signs played in their culture.

When Wittgenstein explains how people from totally different cultures are able to understand each other, he refers to 'the common behaviour of mankind'.[3] There are, nevertheless, also behaviours common to humans and animals, which enable a form of communication. However, Wittgenstein also emphasizes that people, simply because of their cultural differences, can be incomprehensible to each other – and it will not necessarily help if they speak the same language; just before his remark about the lion, Wittgenstein writes:

> We also say of some people that they are transparent to us. It is, however, important as regards this observation that one human being can be a complete enigma to another. We learn this when we come into a strange country with entirely strange traditions; and, what is more, even given a mastery of the country's language. We do not *understand* the people. (And not because of not knowing what they are saying to themselves.) We cannot find our feet with them.[4]

Something about these people can be understood of course, especially the activities we have in common, but there will be aspects of their way of life that we are unable to penetrate. Why would this not function similarly with animals? There are a number of activities we share with lions, like eating or relaxing, and it's not impossible to understand these activities. Even some of the activities we do not share with lions can be understood. I have never crept up behind a gazelle to sink my teeth into it, but I have no real problem understanding this activity. Perhaps what we really should say is: 'If a lion could speak, we would not understand *all* that it says.' Or: 'If a lion could speak, we would understand *some* of what it said.' None of these rewordings, however, capture Wittgenstein's point.

Is it simply that language is what separates us from all other animals? That having a language changes everything, so that a lion that could speak just as we humans do, would not have a lion consciousness? If that were the case it would no longer be a lion. Perhaps we ought to say: 'If a lion could speak, it would not understand itself.' Or rather: 'If a lion could speak, it would not understand what it's like to be a regular lion, that cannot speak.'

Something like this is the case with Franz Kafka's fictitious character Red Peter, the protagonist in his short story 'A Report to an Academy' (1917).[5] Red Peter is an ape with the ability to speak human language, who has been asked by a German academy to tell them about his life. The academy members are not least excited to hear Red Peter tell them about how it is to be an ape in its natural state, prior to the acquisition of its language. However, Red Peter must regretfully tell them that he cannot report on that because his recollections of being an ape have been erased during the process of learning human language and mannerisms. He has simply forgotten what it's like to be an ape. All he does is describe the process from being caught until his present success as an entertainer who smokes, drinks red wine and speaks like a typical European.

Before Kafka wrote his short story, philosophers had considered the possibility of talking apes. Immanuel Kant said that people were the only beings that actually have the ability to speak, but he allowed for the fact that evolution might continue in such a way that humans are no longer alone in their capability for language and intelligence, and that chimpanzees and orang-utans might also gain the ability to speak and understand.[6] Julien Offray de La Mettrie claimed, in his famous work *Man a Machine*, from 1748, that an ape can be trained to learn a language – and this ape will then be neither a 'wild' nor inferior human, but more like a human being just like all other humans.[7] The language makes all the difference.

When Red Peter reports to the academy, five years have passed since he was trapped while drinking water from a river, then caged and transported to Germany. During the long crossing he had plenty of time to speculate, and noticed that the people on board the ship were allowed to go about freely while he sat in an uncomfortable cage. He thought that if he could imitate humans, it would bring him a similar freedom. The ape wanted to become human by mimicking humans. It was amazingly easy, he says. He saw that humans shook hands and he imitated them. Then he learned to spit, and that was easy too. It was more difficult to learn to smoke tobacco and drink alcohol, however, but it was possible. One day he drank a whole bottle of gin at once, and something happened to him: suddenly he called out 'Hello!' It was there and then, by breaking into the human language, that he broke down the barrier between humans and animals, and became part of the human community. People were quite simply talking apes.

In the five years that have elapsed, Red Peter has gone through such huge changes that his own 'ape-ness' has become just as alien to him as the audience's 'ape-ness' was for them. By becoming a talking ape, and so a human being, he has lost touch with what it was to be an ape that could not speak. In short, an ape who could speak would no longer be an ape, just as a talking lion can no longer be a lion. Where Wittgenstein's lion cannot be understood by us, Kafka's ape cannot understand himself because he has become one of us. What about 'talking' apes in the real world?

TWO

Language

Most attempts to teach animals language have naturally been made during the study of chimpanzees. This is not so strange, since there is good reason to assume that they have the best prerequisites for learning one. There are areas in the chimpanzee's brain that correspond to the language areas of the human brain, but they are quite small. First, attempts were made to teach the chimpanzees spoken language, but of course that didn't work simply because chimpanzees lack the speech mechanisms that humans have. The next step was to teach them sign language. A chimpanzee called Washoe was the first to manage this, and he has been followed by a number of other chimpanzees, and some gorillas and orang-utans. Another approach was to teach chimpanzees to press keys with different symbols.[1] Some of the most famous of these 'talking' apes are Washoe, who managed to learn 132 characters in five years; Nim, 125 characters in three-and-a-half years; and Koko the gorilla, who learned 250 characters in four years. Chimpanzees who have learned sign language have been observed using it when communicating with each other, despite being unaware that humans are watching them. To gauge how impressive this is, it needs to be mentioned that a human two-year-old, by comparison, learns about ten words each day. Teaching an ape to use signs and symbols is laborious work. Small human children do it with ease.

What do these primates say with the signs they use? So far, no signing ape has been able to say anything noteworthy about what it's like to be an ape. Mostly they ask for food and drink, but requests for play and cuddling are also common. Washoe, Koko and the other primates managed to learn a relatively large number of signs and were able to communicate with them, but they acquired no understanding of grammar. Countless other species, such as dogs, rats and pigeons, have also learned to link a sign – such as a light or a movement – to an action; and it has not been shown convincingly that the ape-language of Washoe and Koko is any different qualitatively from this type of associative learning. If you look at what the 'talking' apes say, it is mostly 'get food', 'get orange', 'get banana'. Nim, who was one of the stars in this field, made by far the longest continuous statement with the following remark: 'Give orange me give eat orange me eat orange give me eat orange give me you.'[2] In comparison, a human two-year-old is able to use nouns, verbs, prepositions and so on, in a grammatically correct manner. They can also talk about things other than what's right in front of them at that moment. One can ask what it means that an ape can use sign language to ask for things – because they undoubtedly can. It might seem to differ slightly from pushing a button or pulling a lever to get a banana. In short, it is a long way from what we would normally consider to be competent language use.

Numerous researchers have claimed that animals, trained by themselves, have produced far more sophisticated pronouncements, giving detailed accounts of life and death, telling jokes and so on; but when other researchers have examined this material, there turns out to be quite a large gap between what the animals have literally said using signs, and the interpretations their instructors have made. In short, there seems to be a significant degree of over-interpretation. Independent researchers found a much lower proportion of meaningful signs and sign combinations. One could say this is due to the fact that the independent researchers did not know the animals that well, and consequently did not have such good prerequisites for interpreting them. Obviously, the signs used by the animals need to be interpreted; but the further one has to stray from a literal rendering of what they actually communicated with the signs – in order to achieve a coherent message – the more likely it is that this message will become the interpreter's construction rather than what was originally intended by the animal using the sign. The instructors have a greater will than the independent researchers to interpret characters used in transposed meaning or similar, when the sign appears to have been used incorrectly. A much-discussed example is that of Koko the gorilla who – while being a little uncooperative one day – was asked to show the sign for drinking, and after a lot of ifs and buts, pointed to her ear instead of her mouth. Koko's instructor interpreted this as a joke from Koko's side, while sceptics were more inclined to think that Koko had simply made a mistake. In general, one might say that the more effort needed to make such favourable interpretations, the less convincing it is that these animals have any meaningful understanding of language. On the other hand, many of them display quite a good understanding of what is said to them verbally. However, results like this have also faced objections from critics who believe it is problematic that the instructors – whom the animals interact with every single day – are the same ones giving them the verbal messages. The idea is that it can be a bodily hint, not an understanding of language, that produces the desired behaviour. These hints do not necessarily have to be something of which the researchers themselves are conscious. However, it is monstrously difficult to carry out experiments like this without the very researchers the animals are familiar with being present.

There have been extensive discussions about whether apes have or are in any way capable of acquiring a language. There will never be any agreement over this question, but the pendulum seems to swing towards most researchers believing that apes do not have language, at least not what linguists would normally call language. Some individual animals have learned various signs, albeit fewer than what a normal human three-year-old can manage. An ape's communication is fascinating, but highly limited. Even the most highly trained primates, who have learned a significant number of characters and symbols, are unable to learn elementary grammar. No chimpanzee is going to write a great novel. One might imagine that a descendant of the chimpanzee could one day manage it, but a being like that will have evolved so much that it would no longer be a chimpanzee.

The answer to the question of whether animals have languages is of course not clear. It depends on what your requirement is for calling something a language. If you have a very broad concept of language, where 'language' becomes more or less synonymous with 'communication', it is obvious that a very large number of animals do have languages since a very large number of animals obviously communicate. For example, the Austrian ethologist Karl von Frisch was awarded the Nobel Prize in 1973 for showing that bees communicate through dance, and that this dance can even be separated into different 'dialects'. However, if you have a narrow understanding of languages, where X is a language if, and only if, it contains so-called recursive structures, it is more likely that animals have no language. By recursive it is meant that a phrase may contain another phrase of the same kind such as: 'I know you think your dog understands what you think.' In an influential article, linguist Noam Chomsky, and biologists Marc Hauser and W. Tecumseh Fitch, claimed that recursive structures like these are only found in human communication.[3] Critics have tried to point out these structures in other animal species, including in birdsong, but there is little to suggest that any other animal has a communication system that uses them. If something must have such a structure in order to be called a language, then based on that judgement we humans would be the only animals with language. Personally I do not believe that we can provide necessary and sufficient conditions for something being a language, but I am inclined to place myself at the more restrictive end of the understanding of languages.

Having said that, is it really important whether we can refer to animal communication as 'language' or not? It is undeniably true that they communicate. Other species are clearly able to communicate feelings and intentions to each other and to us. Animals communicate both with their own species and with foreign species. A gazelle that notices a lion stalking it will often leap high into the air. This tells the lion that it has been seen, and that it will never manage to catch the gazelle. Then they can both avoid wasting lots of energy on a hunt that will not lead to anything. My dog can without doubt communicate to me that she is hungry and wants food, that she needs a pee and wants to go out for a walk, or that she is afraid and wants protection. Not least, she can express great pleasure when someone in the family comes home; then she will make distinctive sounds that alternate from a deep rumble to high and bright tones – and can perhaps be described as 'wowowowowowowooooouuuuuu'. It's quite clear to me that when Luna makes this sound and her tail beats like a drumstick, she simply has to be described as very, very happy. There is enormous joy being expressed through 'wowowowo-wowooooouuuuuu'. At the same time, her communication skills are admittedly quite limited. For example, she has no ability to use symbols. That is: if I chose to be extremely charitable, I could say that Luna uses her toy bird – which she always fetches and makes squeaking noises with when someone comes home – as a symbol of her happiness, but that might be stretching it too far.

No other animal has the linguistic capabilities we have. They have a much smaller register than us. One could argue that they may have a register we do not have and that might be true in itself, but one important difference is that communication between animals seems to be quite strictly bound to what is around them at that present time, while we also have the ability to communicate about the past and the future. For example, I can talk about events that happened when I was a child, or our holiday last year; I can also talk about events which are yet to occur, such as going to Beijing in late summer. Animal communication, on the other hand, is essentially limited to their immediate surroundings – their communicative spaces consist of the here and now.

Animals are without doubt expressive. Not all animals, of course, but many. They have different types of expressiveness. For example, a cat uses very little mimicry in its face compared to a dog, but it will communicate with sound and with the rest of its body. This expressiveness is impressed upon us in a completely different way from that of other natural objects, and it demands a response from us. Humans have such a large, expressive repertoire between us that we can readily understand what others are expressing, even when we do not share a language or where the language is totally absent. When my father was on a respirator for several weeks, unable to talk or write, I understood him most of the time if he was thirsty or had pain, or the support socks he wore to prevent blood clots were too tight. We humans also share a significant expressive repertoire with many animals. It is not the case that we normally look at a certain animal's behaviour, then refer to an interpretation chart of what this behaviour indicates, and then make a decision as to what the animal's state of mind should be. That is to say, we can always divide the process of understanding into these three stages – and then our understanding of other humans would have to be looked at in the same way. However, our experience of what we do when we understand an animal's behaviour is not broken down like that. Understanding of an animal's state of mind has a completely different immediacy from that, especially when it concerns animals we know well.

Of course, we can be mistaken about the states of mind of both animals and humans, and it is therefore important to be aware that the immediacy of understanding is not synonymous with its infallibility. Any understanding holds the possibility for misunderstanding. The misunderstandings decrease the more we are in the company of those we want to understand, whether they are animals or humans. With animals that we do not share as much of an expressive repertoire with, it becomes more difficult. The Pacific octopus can be a telling example. It is an explosion of signs, but we are simply unable to find anything meaningful in most of them. It may be that there is something meaningful there which we are unable to grasp, but it could also be that there is no meaning there to be understood – that it is simply a fascinating display of colour. Nevertheless, we have to say that, to the extent that we can acknowledge behaviour as expressive, we can in principle also recognize the state of mind that this behaviour expresses.

Many philosophers have perceived the relationship between language and thinking as so close that the capacity for language has been regarded as a necessary and sufficient condition for the ability to think. Conversely, the lack of language skills has been regarded as a sufficient condition for the lack of ability to think. This has probably been an important reason why some philosophers have been more willing to consider computers to be capable of thinking than animals, since computers undoubtedly have a form of language. This reasoning is, in my opinion, absurd because so many animals obviously demonstrate consciousness – and the ability to think – while in my opinion it is doubtful if any computer ever will. If it is true that one can only think by virtue of having a natural language, beings without such a language cannot think. However, it is more plausible to assert that a number of animals – and infants, for that matter – show clear signs of thinking, which is therefore why the thesis of language as a precondition for thinking is doubtful. That language is a precondition for many forms of thinking is one thing, but that there should be a precondition for every kind of thinking is something else.

Philosophers have had a tendency to overestimate the significance of language. After all, pretty advanced thinking can take place in organisms that have no language in the normal sense of the word. Just imagine a group of chimpanzees, where there is a complex social system with hierarchies and alliances, and each chimpanzee must act with care according to where he or she is positioned in the social system. It seems unreasonable to claim that the behaviour of a chimpanzee – which orients itself in this complex system – cannot at least be partly explained by the presence of thought. Language is a medium for thought, and it is an exceptionally powerful medium but, as mentioned, certainly not the only medium. Humans have linguistic and symbolic resources that other animals do not possess. Our ability to form symbols gives us a degree of independence in our relationship with the world, in that we can replace objects with symbols for the same objects.[4] Our thoughts have a far greater potential scope than any other animal can know, purely because we are an *animal symbolicum*. It also gives our feelings another playroom. A human might fall in love with or be in the deepest fear of a person they have never even met, someone perhaps even situated on another continent.

Numerous animals can communicate in a referential manner where they use signals – especially sounds – to refer to certain objects that are separate from others. In other words, they can draw distinctions between different objects, and communicate this to others. They can not only use a signal for 'danger', but signal what *kind* of danger it is, whether it be a bird, a snake or a cat. Some animals have distinct signals for each of these, while others use a combination of signals. And we can, at least partly, understand what they say.

Wittgenstein quotes Goethe's *Faust*: 'In the beginning was the deed.'[5] Language is, as Wittgenstein says, a refinement. In actions we find a regularity, and without such a regularity, understanding can never take place. He describes this regularity as 'the common behaviour of mankind'.[6] We must then consider the full range of human actions.[7] However, there are not only common behaviours of mankind, but behaviours we have in common with other animals. With a foundation like this we can understand animals, even though they do not have a language.

THREE

Seeing Animal Consciousness

'The human body is the best picture of the human soul.'[1] Wittgenstein's claim about the relationship between body and soul in humans can also be extended to animals: 'If one sees the behaviour of a living thing, one sees its soul.'[2] Nothing supernatural is implied by the word 'soul' here. Seeing a soul means seeing *somebody*, someone with a subjectivity or consciousness, and not a mere thing. There is an immediacy in our perception of the other, and in perceiving that he has a soul or is conscious. This can be illustrated by considering a person who, for example, has slipped on the ice and crashed to the ground with their arm twisted and bent. We would not look at that person and think: 'A person writhing and screaming like that would usually be in a state of pain, so there is good reason to assume that the person I am now looking at is feeling pain.' We would carry out no such deduction, but rather *see* the pain from the person's behaviour. We are even less likely to think: 'I cannot know if he's in pain, because his feelings are just something that exists within him, beyond what I can recognize.'[3] To see the soul that Wittgenstein writes about is not about being able to look through a kind of shell – instead it is simply the fact that *seeing* this body and its behaviour *is* to see a soul. However, this assumes that what we are seeing has a sufficient resemblance to ourselves. For example, we can only say that an animal has pain when it exhibits a behaviour that resembles human behaviour.

You cannot *know* that your dog has a consciousness and that it thinks, but you have more reason to assume it does, than not. Many animals *indicate* so clearly that they have a consciousness, that it cannot be said there is room for *reasonable* doubt. This applies not least to all mammals. However, the animal world is diverse, and there is reason to doubt that crustaceans have a consciousness, and also cases where there is no doubt at all, such as oysters. If we now limit ourselves to mammals, one can say that a person who does not *see* the animal's consciousness, that it has feelings and intentions, suffers from what Wittgenstein calls 'aspect-blindness'. According to Wittgenstein, aspect-blindness is akin to being tone-deaf.[4] A tone-deaf person will receive the same sounds as someone with perfect pitch, but will not *hear* the same, and an aspect-blind person will receive the same visual stimuli, but will not *see* the same as someone capable of seeing aspects. There is a dimension of meaning that is lost on the aspect-blind.

If a dog is seen standing at an entranceway, scratching the door and whining, you can always insist that you do not *know* what the dog wants, or if it has any consciousness and the ability to want anything. One can always be sceptical of these things while sitting at a desk, but I would absolutely recommend getting up from the desk and taking the dog out for a walk, if you are to spare it discomfort. For all intents and purposes, it is obvious that the dog needs to pee and wants to go out, since it has learned that it has to pee outside. When you return to your desk after walking with the dog, who quite rightly made a large puddle as soon as you got outdoors, that kind of sceptical speculation seems a little nonsensical. David Hume describes the feeling of being drawn more and more into such speculation, where you no longer know right from left about anything, and how you leave speculations aside for some reason or other and then do something else:

> I dine, I play a game of backgammon, I converse, and am merry with my friends; and when after three or four hours' amusement, I would return to these speculations, they appear so cold, and strained, and ridiculous, that I cannot find in my heart to enter into them any further.[5]

The expressive acts of animals are, like the expressions of human beings, there from the beginning. They are there as part of what we grow up in, acquire a language in, and teach ourselves awareness in. It is not the case that I first get to know myself and then on that basis deduce that other people also have a consciousness. The awareness of another's consciousness is at least as primordial as the awareness of my own. That also applies to awareness of an animal's consciousness. An animal's intentions are normally immediately understandable. As Wittgenstein writes: 'What is the natural expression of an intention? – Look at a cat when it stalks a bird; or a beast when it wants to escape.'[6] We learn to understand an animal's intentions by dealing with them. For anyone who has grown up with animals, the accusation that there is something suspicious about attributing the same intentions to animals is a bit odd. The reason for this is that the critics seem to assume that one first learns to understand another's intentions when dealing with humans, but then does something questionable by extending this to include animals. However, anyone who has grown up with both animals and humans has usually learned to understand the intentions of others – both animals and humans – by interacting with both animals and humans.

I know that a person who smiles and laughs warmly is happy because I learned what 'happy' means by referring to this sort of criteria. Similarly, I know that a person who sits and cries is sad, because that is what I have learned 'sad' means. There are no inferences here. I do not think: 'I observe that he is sobbing, and therefore I have reason to assume that he is sad.' On the contrary, I *see* that he is sad when he is sobbing. More complex conditions, such as grief or loneliness, which go beyond mere sadness, will have more complex criteria. In any case, the understanding of internal processes will always require external criteria.[7] The point is not that pain is identical to pain behaviour or that grief is the same as grief behaviour, but rather that we can explain expressions that denote mental conditions only by referring to external observable signs. We *see* feelings. We don't see contractions in someone's face and then infer that the person feels joy or sadness.[8]

Here, a sceptical voice might sneak up on you and say, 'You don't *know* that he is really sad. Maybe he's just acting like it. Or maybe he's just a robot. But you know very well if you have pain yourself."[9] You can always *say* it, but I doubt if you can *live* with such scepticism. Is this really a doubt that you would be inclined to articulate if you saw the person mentioned – who has slipped on the ice and is screaming with their arm twisted and bent? Not at all. Feelings are not only hidden, purely mental phenomena – they are also behaviours, actions and expressions that are visible. They exist in faces and gestures, they are not hidden behind them.

The French phenomenologist Maurice Merleau-Ponty highlights the close connection between a feeling and its physical expression. The feeling is not something which lies behind the gesture, but is contained *in* the gesture. Merleau-Ponty states:

> Faced with an angry or threatening gesture, I have no need, in order to understand it, to recall the feelings which I myself experienced when I used these gestures on my own account . . . I do not see anger or a threatening attitude as a psychic fact hidden behind the gesture, I read anger in it. The gesture *does not make me think* of anger, it is anger itself.[10]

Of course, this does not mean that we would be unable to hide a feeling or that a hidden feeling is not 'real', but the hidden feeling presupposes the explicit one.

There is something 'within' both humans and animals, but this inner space is not normally hidden – on the contrary, it is highly visible. As a rule, I can *see* you are happy or sad. The 'inner' can also be hidden, such as when someone does their utmost to maintain a mask instead of expressing how sad they are about something. However, it is not hidden because it is something 'inner' – but rather because they are consciously showing a different face to the one that would be the normal expression of their inner condition. This expression may well fool others too, for better or worse.

The point is that the exact same things we take into consideration about human mental conditions can also be applied to animals. However, the criteria become increasingly uncertain the further we get from the situation in which we learned to detect them. For animals that have a very different life form from ours, it would be much more difficult to decide what the criteria for happiness or sadness is. Yet the same will be applicable when considering people from foreign cultures. Merleau-Ponty considers the feelings, the expressions and the relationships between them to be flexible. He points out that the expressions of different feelings vary from culture to culture, and that also implies there is a variation in the feeling itself. As he sees it, it is impossible to distinguish between a 'natural' and a 'conventional' level among the feelings and expressions of humans – the natural and the conventional overlap seamlessly with each other.

You also need context in order to understand. If you see a small child crying, you can ask yourself if it is crying because it is hurt, or because it is scared. It is impossible to say without knowing the context in which the crying occurs. The same is true of animal behaviour – there you must also know the context in order to understand. As Wittgenstein points out: 'If someone behaves such-and-such, in such-and-such circumstances, we say that the person concerned is sad.' And he adds: 'We also say this about dogs.'[11] Wittgenstein emphasizes that many of our mental concepts are also applicable to animals.[12] Because of the similarities to human behaviour, we say that animals can be happy, angry, afraid, sad, surprised or hesitant, that they can notice something, investigate it or think something. We will say that some animals are capable of considering something or changing their minds. It is funny how cats almost always stop just before the doorstep, as though they have to consider it more thoroughly: 'Should I really go out or stay in?' A dog will normally run straight out without any hesitation. It may well run back in again, but there is very little hesitation at the doorstep itself. It does not seem too much of a stretch to use terms like 'weigh up' or 'change one's mind' here. All of these concepts are derived from the psychological repertoire of humans, and it is totally legitimate to use them to describe animals. In some cases it is unclear which terms are appropriate and which ones are not – because they are so strongly linked to human characteristics. Two examples of this can be loneliness and boredom. At the same time, as Wittgenstein also points out, it is little wonder that some of our mental concepts are only applicable to beings that command a language.[13] For example, I cannot describe my dog as 'honest' for the simple reason that it cannot be dishonest. The concepts of honesty and dishonesty do not apply to her life. Nor can she be described as envious. Either way, the ability to use a language is only one type of behaviour among others.

If I say that Luna thinks Iben, my daughter, is in the bathroom, behind a closed door, I am not saying that the dog has formulated the sentence 'Iben is in the bathroom' in some kind of inner language – but simply that she behaves in a similar manner to how a person, with a similar level of comprehension, could or would have behaved. When I ascribe to her the belief that Iben is in the bathroom, it is not because I want to be a mind-reader with privileged access to Luna's consciousness, but simply for the trivial reason that she behaves as though she thinks Iben is in bathroom. The more we know about the animal – from species-defined traits of mannerisms and senses, to the individual traits of the specific animal – the more reliable these ascribings of perceptions are. It is more reliable when there is a greater resemblance between our species and most reliable when we ascribe perceptions to our own species, other humans, to whom we are most similar and know best.

If we discard the idea of consciousness as something hidden, something that can only be revealed by language – like the ability to break through the barrier separating the internal from the external – and instead recognize that the internal is *visible* in what is external, there is no extraordinary difficulty in ascribing different states of consciousness to animals. This does not mean there will not, in practice, be interpretation problems, because we do not always know how to understand a behaviour, but the problem is not that the internal is 'hidden'.

When we use our own experiences as a basis for understanding what is going on in the consciousness of another animal, we must assume that there is a fairly systematic link between behaviour and awareness reflected in the two species. In addition, we can draw on knowledge from the relationship between neurology and consciousness – but the neurological path is, in my opinion, less illuminating than the behavioural one.

The American psychologist Gregory Berns claims, in his book *What It's Like to Be a Dog*, to have solved the problem of knowing the animal mind.[14] You just have to train the dog to lie still in an fMRI machine that tells us which areas of the brain are active and at what time. The problem with this kind of approach is not only that Berns believes that one gains a kind of direct access to the first-person perspective by studying the brain, but also because the brain is itself something 'external' in relation to consciousness. Can we, for example, see a dog's happiness more directly by looking at the active areas in its brain than by seeing it wagging its tail? I would say that the dog's happiness is manifestly more visible, more accessible, in how it moves, than by what areas of its brain are more activated in particular situations.

We have limited knowledge about the relationship between the brain and consciousness, but we know that the changes in the brain are accompanied by changes in consciousness, and vice versa. This does not mean that we can, just like that, say the brain and consciousness are identical. A brain has no consciousness, but the *dog* has a consciousness. The brain is undoubtedly a crucial prerequisite in order for the dog to have a consciousness, but that is all. All states of consciousness must have a neurological foundation, and this is something that can be established by the fact that damage to a particular area in the brain will lead to loss of a particular consciousness function. We know, for example, that injuries in the areas of the human brain called Wernicke's area and Broca's area lead to a loss of linguistic understanding and linguistic formulation. This does not mean that linguistic ability may be reduced to a particular state in particular parts of the brain. The problem is that while we possess all the relevant information at a neurological level, we cannot explain all the properties on a psychological level. Each of these levels has its own objects, laws and concepts. The different levels are not completely independent of each other, but they cannot be reduced to each other either. Studies of phenomena on lower levels can illuminate phenomena on higher levels, but only to a limited extent.

Consciousness is dependent on interaction between the brain, the whole body and the body's surroundings. Neurosciences have made great progress, but we also tend to overestimate how much they can tell us, something Berns's book is an example of. Michael S. Gazzaniga, the founder of cognitive neuroscience, and certainly someone in favour of using fMRI scans, points out that there is a widespread 'superstition' about what images of a brain tell us.[15] Among other things, he refers to studies which show that people perceive explanations of psychological phenomena as more credible if accompanied by images of a brain, even when the image has no relevance at all to the explanation. They even perceive scientifically weaker explanations with such images as more credible than more scientifically robust explanations that do not use such images.

Once we have found a neurological correlate for a state of consciousness in humans, and we find a similar neurological state in another species, we cannot easily conclude that it is about the same state of consciousness. A crucial part of the human neurological basis for feeling regret lies in the orbitofrontal cortex, right at the front of the brain. The basis for such an assertion is the observation that stroke patients, with damage to this area, no longer experience remorse after making obviously bad choices; and also because we have seen activity in this area when people who have this part of the brain intact feel regret. We know that the same area in a rat's brain is active when they have chosen an action option that gives a worse reward than another they could have chosen. If the rat's behaviour gives it a worse reward than another behaviour would have done, and if it stops and looks back at the more favourable option, the rat's orbitofrontal cortex becomes activated.[16] Does this mean that the rat feels *regret*? It is difficult to say. For us humans, regret is such a complex phenomenon – so strongly linked to our linguistic abilities, and to an internal monologue about what might have been – that it is hard to imagine that regret is independent of this. For the sake of argument, let us assume that a rat can feel 'regret'. We are then left with the question of what it is a rat feels when it feels 'regret'. Besides it being a form of discomfort, it is difficult to say much about the matter. If rats do have this ability to feel regret, there is reason to assume that it is also found in other mammals, such as cats and dogs. Here I have to admit that I have never observed anything with any of my cats that indicates they have ever regretted anything. They have asked to go outside in bad weather, then asked to be let back in again a minute later. I would call that changing your mind, rather than regret. How about dogs? Perhaps the expression of 'guilt' often attributed to dogs is a form of amoral regret, where the dog does not feel guilty for doing something wrong, but rather a regret for having done something that has caused its owner to be discontented.

Either way, we must look at the animal's *behaviour* when we try to determine the kind of mental abilities that they possess. Studies of their neurology cannot replace the study of their actual behaviour. If one believes that we get some kind of instant access to an animal's awareness by studying their brain images, I cannot see how it differs from me saying to my wife, during an argument: 'I don't quite understand what you mean, but I will now carry out an fMRI scan of your brain, so I *can* understand it.'

FOUR

A Human Form

Anyone who has ever had a pet has asked themselves a question like: 'What's my dog thinking right now?' or 'What's my cat trying to say to me?' We wonder if it is at all possible to understand them, and if they can understand us. For most animal owners, the answer will be a resounding yes: that they both understand their pets and experience a level of understanding from them; that they understand the dog or cat's state of mind; or that the dog or cat has come and comforted them if they have experienced something sad. This is the amateur's way of talking about the animal. 'Amateur', as mentioned, means 'one who loves'. There is an emotional dimension in the amateur's connection to the animal which quickly vanishes in the eyes of a professional. When the amateur talks about an animal, he will typically use terms from human psychology. The amateur will use anthropomorphism in his attempt to understand animals. The term originates from the Greek words *anthropos* (human) and *morphe* (form), meaning to give something a human form or shape. When the amateur describes his dog or cat, he will typically use terms like the dog is 'thinking about something', that it is 'jealous', 'sad' or 'lonely'. Many philosophers and naturalists, however, will systematically try to avoid using such expressions, based on the concept that the animal, as part of the natural world, must be *explained* rather than *understood*. The biologist wants to explain the animal's behaviour, not understand its consciousness. If you were to focus on one particular mortal sin within the modern study of animals, it would be the use of anthropomorphism. The first to use the expression was supposedly the Greek philosopher Xenophanes, who criticized the Homeric poems that described the gods as though they resembled humans. The question is whether we can shape our images of the gods in any way other than by using man as a starting point. The same applies to animals.

In nineteenth-century biology it was common to talk about an animal's feelings and mental life. Charles Darwin was an example of this, writing a great book on it: *The Expression of the Emotions in Man and Animals* (1872). However, there were also negative lessons to be learned from this practice. George Romanes, who was Darwin's research assistant and designated heir to the project, showed just how bad things can go when anthropomorphism is allowed more or less free rein. Romanes told highly imaginative stories of animal behaviour, and he assumed that animals must have had fairly advanced conscious states to have behaved in that way. Among other things, he talks about a monkey that had been shot and had smeared blood all over his hand, to show it to a hunter and give him a bad conscience. There is really no reason to assume that a monkey has any concept of what a 'bad conscience' is, and even less reason to think that it has an understanding of the mental state it may cause in a human when shown the consequences of its actions.

Just as Darwin appointed Romanes his successor, so Romanes appointed C. Lloyd Morgan to be his, and Morgan made it clear that one should limit the kind of fanciful descriptions Romanes had come up with. So he introduced a principle: we should never interpret a behaviour as a product of a higher mental ability if it can be interpreted as the product of a lower one.[1] This means, for example, that if one and the same behaviour can be interpreted as a product both of instinct and of reasoning, then one should give preference to the first, simpler explanation. This principle was the benchmark for animal studies in the twentieth century, where it became increasingly less common to talk about an animal's feelings and mental life. Such talk was often perceived as unscientific. It is worth noting that Morgan himself did not want his principle to be interpreted so rigidly. He believed that there was enough good evidence for ascribing advanced mental capabilities to a range of animals to legitimize describing their behaviour as a product of having these elevated qualities. He supported the idea that animal scientists should use terms and feelings from their own consciousness and that they should consider the animals to be analogous to this. As Morgan interpreted his principle, he was in no doubt that it was reasonable to attribute an advanced consciousness to his dog, but there were also clear limits. He had no doubt that dogs were highly intelligent, but without any capacity for abstract thinking; they certainly had the capacity for empathy, but no idea about fairness. In *Animal Life and Intelligence* (1890–91) he writes:

That dogs feel sympathy with man will scarcely be questioned by any one who has known the companionship of these four-legged friends. At times they seem instinctively to grasp our moods, to be silent with us when we are busy, to lay their shaggy heads on our knees when we are worried or sad, and to be quickened to fresh life when we are happy and glad – so keen are their perceptions.[2]

Morgan's canon was basically a good remedy for anthropomorphism that had gone wild, but unfortunately the drug worked too well, causing an almost parodic resistance to ascribing 'higher' characteristics to animals. The problem was that it prevented the most fundamental consideration one should have when it comes to understanding something, namely to give justice to the phenomenon one has chosen to understand. The zoologist and ethologist Frans de Waal coined the expression 'anthropodenial' to describe this conflict with anthropomorphism.[3] The expression suggests a dismissal of all similarities between humans and animals for no other reason than that it is 'unthinkable' or 'unscientific'.

Nevertheless, the consequence of this stricter interpretation was that animals were essentially regarded as a kind of vending machine of which we could not know the inner life, where stimuli went in and a response came out. In recent decades, the pendulum has swung back, not least since the American biologist Donald Griffin published the book *The Question of Animal Awareness* (1976), which has meant that today there is greater receptiveness to a different principle: we should attribute higher characteristics to animals as long as they are the most reasonable explanation for the animal's behaviour. We can call it a resumption of much of Darwin's project in *The Expression of the Emotions in Man and Animals*. Darwin pointed out that humans and animals have essentially the same senses: sight, hearing, smell, taste and touch. Animals can imitate and remember things. Furthermore, he claimed that animals experience desire and reluctance, pleasure and dejection, just as much as humans. Today, most would agree with him. However, the lessons learned from Romanes's mistakes are still strongly embedded, and most would oppose attributing qualities like generosity and shame to animals as Darwin did.

If I say that my dog is creeping up on a pigeon to catch it, I'm on safe ground because the description does not refer to any of the dog's mental characteristics. I would be even safer if I were to say that the dog is positioning itself so that the pigeon will come within its reach. If, on the other hand, I say that my dog *wants* or *wishes* to catch the pigeon, I am doing something far more problematic because I am then using concepts from our human mental inventory. I might add, by the way, that Luna has never succeeded, and never will succeed, in catching a pigeon. Perhaps by using these concepts of wanting or wishing I am just projecting my own thoughts and emotions onto Luna, because, after all, I cannot know what is happening in her mind. On the other hand, I can know what her behaviour is, simply by observing it. So it may then seem safest to make do with describing her behaviour and refrain from speculations about her mental state. However, this kind of strategy is unsatisfactory; she clearly, and constantly, shows signs of having a consciousness. Her consciousness is just as clear to my eyes as her movements are.

If I say that 'Luna is happy,' then I am ascribing to her a mental capacity derived from a human psychological inventory. I can avoid this by saying: 'Luna behaves in such a way that we would have interpreted it as an expression of happiness had she been a human being.' But that is unnecessarily long-winded and silly. Of course I cannot *know* that Luna-happy corresponds with Lars-happy, but I have good reason to assume it. For that matter, I cannot *know* if what I experience as happiness matches what other people experience as happiness – it is in itself quite conceivable that your happiness is significantly different from mine – but obviously I have better reason to assume that they are more of a match than not. Here, too, there has been a change within biology recently, so that you no longer have to write 'happy' or 'angry' using inverted commas when describing animals. So in that respect, biology has come in line with the amateur view – or common sense, if you will. I wish the same could be said about philosophy.

If your dog is chasing a cat and the cat climbs into a tree while your dog stands barking under the tree, the easiest explanation is that the dog *believes* that the cat is in the tree. At the same time, we are using anthropomorphism here because we are saying something about what the dog 'believes', and consequently using a concept from human psychology. To me it's quite obvious that my dog thinks about many different things, like wanting food or to go out for a walk. Her behaviour clearly indicates that she has an expectation of this, and just like humans, her expectations can turn to shame; for example, when I open the drawer where her treats are with no intention of giving her a treat, but to get something else. It's not unreasonable to use expressions like 'belief' and 'expectation' when I describe my dog. At the same time, it has to be admitted that her imagination is lacking compared with our own. Her thoughts are clearly linked to the present, and she cannot expect me to come home from a trip tomorrow for the simple reason that she has no concept of 'tomorrow'. But she can expect me to come in through the door soon because she recognizes my footsteps on the stairs.

We should be as open as regards animals showing us their feelings and intentions as we are with people doing it, knowing that we humans are different from other animals in several important respects. If you try to describe behaviour without any use of anthropomorphism, you will be left with a collection of descriptions of movements with little meaning or inner context. The use of such 'human' terms creates context, and therefore also meaning. It is the only possible way we can have any understanding of animals at all – by drawing from our own psychology, our own perceptions and feelings. However, it is also crucial that one takes into account the biological explanations when attempting to understand the animal. Then we can prevent anthropomorphisms from running wild, and attributing to the animal every possible human trait when there may be no sustainable basis for certain claims. The goal is to get these two views, the amateur and the scientific, to fit together.

Most animal owners will claim that they actually understand their animals. And they are probably right. In one test, animal owners were asked to describe the moods of dogs and cats based on still images and film clips.[4] These animal owners used anthropomorphism to a large extent in their descriptions. In addition, there was a control group consisting of people without significant experience with animals. To evaluate how well the subjects had succeeded with their descriptions, three ethologists – researchers who study animals in their natural environment – were asked to judge the answers as 'highly plausible', 'plausible' or 'implausible'. It was found that the subjects who had experience with both dogs and cats consistently gave answers that were 'highly plausible'. Those who had experience of only one species scored slightly less, but even the group with no animal experience had quite good results. The amateur view, full of anthropomorphism, matches reasonably well with the professional view.

What is it like to be a dog? It is a strange question. What is it like to be a human? Are these questions essentially different? One major difference is that I have experience of being human, but not of being a dog. What if I were to ask: what it is like to be a woman? Or Swedish? Or a plumber, tennis pro, primary school teacher or nurse? I have no experience of being any of these. One difference is that the woman, the Swede, the plumber, the tennis pro, the primary school teacher and the nurse can tell me what it is like, using normal verbal language. The dog can communicate what it's like to be a dog, but only to a far lesser degree. In many cases, I understand its preferences by interpreting the sound of its bark, its posture or where it goes when I move. I can see what captures its interest, what makes it happy or it is frustrated or amazed by, but I cannot interview the dog and ask it about how it perceives itself and the world around it.

I can understand the dog by interpreting its behaviour, and I have to view the dog as analogous with myself and consider how it would be for me to be in the situation the dog is now in. On the other hand, I have to take into account that the dog is, after all, a dog and not a person. There are good reasons why, for example, we look at learning to read and write as a right for people, and not for dogs. One can argue that all animal species live in their 'own' world, in a sense. Taking that into consideration, we would never be able to understand an animal of another species. The animal would live in his world, and we in ours. However, the borders between these worlds are porous, allowing us to partly enter the world of other species.

We must then begin with the similarities between the animal's behaviour and our own. If the behaviour is similar, it is basically not unreasonable to assume that the state of consciousness that underlies the behaviour is also similar. David Hume writes:

> 'Tis from the resemblance of the external actions of animals to those we ourselves perform, that we judge their internal likewise to resemble ours; and the same principle of reasoning, carry'd one step farther, will make us conclude that since our internal actions resemble each other, the causes, from which they are deriv'd, must also be

resembling. When any hypothesis, therefore, is advanc'd to explain a mental operation which is common to men and beasts, we must apply the same hypothesis to both.[5]

From this starting point he draws the conclusion that 'no truth appears to me more obvious than that beasts are endow'd with thought and reason as well as men.' However, it has been usual to show greater scepticism here, and claim that we need more positive evidence from another species in order to attribute these qualities to animals.

Why do we have higher demands for proving that animals are conscious and capable of thinking than we do for humans? Humans have language, one can say, and language is proof of consciousness. However, language cannot fully explain this discrepancy because we also ascribe consciousness to people without language, such as young children who have not yet developed a language. If we were as strict when studying the abilities of pre-linguistic children as we are when studying animals, we would not attribute much consciousness to them. The point is not that we need to tighten the requirements for attributing consciousness to humans – it would be absurd if we all had to continually assure ourselves that the people around us are *truly* conscious – but rather that we need more generosity regarding animals. We should not require irrefutable proof, just substantiation.

One can also defend the use of anthropomorphism without having to assume anything at all about what kind of consciousness an animal has. The American philosopher Daniel Dennett has done this by claiming that it is simply a fruitful strategy for explaining and predicting behaviour.[6] Dennett does not care about whether my dog 'wants' or 'expects' food when it comes running at hearing the sound of the food cupboard opening. Whether the dog has any ability to want or expect is irrelevant. What is important is that, by referring to the dog in this way, we can explain its behaviour – that it comes running; and predict future behaviour – that it will also come running the next time it hears this sound. So you can explain and predict actual behaviour by describing the dog *as if* it has these states of consciousness. Nevertheless, we would rather have something more than just an 'as if'. We want to know if the dog really has these states of consciousness. Dennett dismisses this as a meaningless task. On that point, I have to say I disagree. We can no more *prove* that a dog has a consciousness, with perceptions and preferences, than we can prove a human has one, but we have far better reasons to presume so than the opposite.

FIVE

Mind-reading

Humans are good mind-readers. So good, in fact, that we even manage to read thoughts where there are no thoughts to be read. In a well-known psychological study from the 1940s, 34 subjects were shown a short film of a surface where a large triangle, a small triangle and a small circle move around a rectangular shape that they can go in and out of.[1] The subjects were asked to describe what they saw, and all of them, apart from one, described the characters as if they were conscious and had intentions. The reason they did this was because otherwise they would only have had a slightly chaotic stream of images where some geometric figures move arbitrarily. It would simply not provide any significant meaning. By looking at the characters as if they had a consciousness, the subjects could, for example, interpret the film as a love story. One interpretation of the experiment is that the more unpredictable something is, the more inclined we are to attribute to it a consciousness and a purpose, because we can then put this apparently random behaviour into a context that makes sense to us.

We have a highly developed ability to reflect on what is happening in the minds of others. In psychology, this phenomenon is often referred to as 'mentalization'. One can argue that this is one of our most important characteristics as a species because it is a prerequisite for real social intelligence. However, this characteristic also has a tendency to run wild, so we might, for example, interpret a behaviour as an expression of consciousness where there is no consciousness. We can also interpret objects that exhibit no agency at all, if by 'agency' we mean the ability for self-movement, as if they had it. An example of this might be when we get angry with a computer or car that does not work properly, screaming insults at them even though it is obvious that they have no consciousness.

Sometimes we make the opposite mistake, and do not attribute a consciousness to a being when in reality it has one. Until the 1980s it was common to perform surgery on infants without anaesthesia. One reason for this was the increased risk when anaesthetizing infants, and it was also argued that the infant's ability to experience pain was so small – or nonexistent – that it was unnecessary to take such a risk. Today it is widely agreed that infants have a well-developed ability to feel pain, and therefore anaesthesia is also normally given during procedures presumed to be painful. How could the doctors make such a mistake? The infants, after all, showed behaviour indicating they were in pain. The doctors were able to see it, but they interpreted the behaviour as though it was not a genuine expression of pain awareness, because of other perceptions they had about infants.

Similar conclusions have been reached by philosophers that have written about animals, most notoriously perhaps the French

philosopher René Descartes (1596–1650). Descartes acknow-
ledges that there are many similarities when comparing human
actions and animal behaviour, but he claims that this does not
tell us anything about any 'inner actions'. Similarity in external
behaviour is not evidence of similarity in inner life.[2] Animals do
not respond when asked questions, and their behaviour has a
greater regularity than that found in humans.[3] Descartes believed
that the only sure sign of consciousness is language, and conversely, that a lack of language was a strong indication of a lack
of consciousness.[4] He also claims that if you accept that one
animal thinks, you must accept that all animals think, including
oysters and sponges, but since it is absurd to think that oysters
and sponges think, we must conclude that no animal thinks.[5] In
one letter he writes that animals do not see the world as we normally do, but rather in a way that reminds us of how we see the
world when we are absent-minded, where light hits our retinas
and can cause our bodies to move without our being conscious
of it happening.[6] This might lead us to think that he believes animals have a consciousness, but cannot make themselves conscious
that they have consciousness. It would, nevertheless, be stretching the analogy with spiritually absent humans too far, because
his view on the matter is that animals have no consciousness
whatsoever. The animal is simply considered a vending machine
where external stimuli cause behaviour without any awareness
being involved. Pain, according to Descartes, is a conscious phenomenon accompanied by body movements; but in animals
it is only the movement itself, not the corresponding state of

consciousness, that is playing out.[7] He accepts that animals have the same physiological prerequisites for feeling pain as humans, but they lack awareness of the pain. In a letter to Henry More in 1649, Descartes writes that, although he finds it well established that it cannot be proven that animals have a capacity for thought, it has not thereby been proven that animals do *not* have a capacity for thought, since 'the human mind does not reach into their hearts.'[8] So a tiny grain of doubt is present. Descartes' peculiar view of animals cannot be explained by the fact that he had no experience with animals, because he had a little dog called Monsieur Gras, whom he was apparently very fond of and who accompanied him on his walks.

The Cartesian view of animals had a long lifespan. For example, the French physiologist Claude Bernard (1813–1878) performed vivisection (from the Latin *vivus*, meaning 'living', and *secare*, 'cut') on a number of dogs and cats without anaesthesia. He cut them up, and their screams of pain and attempts to wriggle free were of little concern because they were no more than machines. On one occasion his wife and daughters returned home and saw, to their horror, that the family dog had been subjected to this treatment. Of course, the marriage couldn't last, and after the couple had separated his wife became an avid campaigner against cruelty to animals. For Bernard himself, this was just cheap sentimentality that should not get in the way of scientific progress.

Similar thoughts can be found today. The American philosopher Peter Carruthers claims that animals simply lack consciousness, and therefore cannot feel pain at all, so we should stop all these feelings of sympathy we have for them.[9] He represents a modern version of the Stoic view of animals. The Stoic philosophers in ancient times claimed that animals were nothing more than wandering meals. In fact, they believed that animals had no senses at all. This is linked to their view on recognition. For example, they believed that to see a cat is to judge, based on what is provided by the senses, that what you see is a cat. But this judgement can be made only if you have the ability to speak. Since a dog does not have the ability to speak, it cannot *see* a *cat*, even though it has its eyes aimed at a cat. The lack of language will therefore mean that animals cannot be understood, only explained, because there is no psychological life there to understand.

The type of reluctance many philosophers have had – and that many still have to attributing consciousness and thinking to animals – is strange. I have no doubt that the dogs and cats that I have lived with think. However, it is not always clear to me *what* they think. This also applies to the people I have lived with, from childhood to adulthood, and sometimes I don't even know what I am thinking. Nevertheless, there are differences between these three cases. Mostly, I am so immediately present in myself that there is no room for doubt about what is happening in my consciousness. I can be present in my own thoughts and feelings in a way like no other, neither human nor animal. It is an immediacy in the experience of one's self. If I am at a concert and the music being performed really hits me, it's a feeling that resonates in my whole body and mind. It feels incredibly meaningful, without me being able to say clearly what that meaning consists of. I can look at the person beside me, and it may be an old friend whom I know inside out, whom I have listened to the band with since we were teenagers; and I look at his smile, the look on his face and the gestures showing that the music hits him just as deeply, so that we are able to share the experience. Nevertheless, we will never share it completely for the simple reason that I cannot transport myself into his consciousness. The experience will always have a private quality that cannot be shared with anyone else. I *am* in my own thoughts and experiences in a way that no other person can ever be.

As mentioned already, there is something essential about the way other people behave that causes me to see them as conscious. They are *not* first and foremost seen as extended bodies which behave in such a manner that we conclude that they are conscious. Instead, we immediately see them as conscious. Normally, I can understand them almost instantly as well, although sometimes there are those who deliberately hide what is going on in their heads. We all have thoughts and feelings which we do not share with others because we do not want to acknowledge having them. However, we can usually tell how another person is feeling, simply by *looking* at them; and if we are unsure, we are able to ask each other, and get a fairly clear answer. It is different with animals.

We cannot simply ask animals about what they are thinking or feeling, and it's not always easy interpreting their body language. However, by interacting with animals, one can develop interpretative skills. For example, people used to interacting with dogs cannot have failed to notice that tail-wagging often, but not always, means that the dog is happy. Tail-wagging can have a number of different meanings, depending on whether it is slow or fast, pointed more to the right or left, and relative to the situation. Dog owners will most often learn to interpret their dog without thinking so carefully about it. However, those same people may regret using these interpretations when encountering a cat. Anyone viewing calm tail-wagging as an expression of friendliness or pleasure, rather than irritation, runs the imminent risk of getting their hands scratched. When a dog places its head in your lap, you can be certain that it is a sign of affection. Were an elephant to attempt the same, you'd be advised to get away as quickly as possible, because it is trying to kill you by crushing you with its forehead.

There is a significant difference between my experience of myself and my experience of others. My experience of myself is an experience that is given both externally and internally, while I can experience only what is external in others. The elephant example shows that none of us are mind-readers, strictly speaking. We cannot simply see the elephant's intentions without knowing a little about elephant behaviour. All we are provided with is the body of the elephant and the movements and sounds it makes. We can immediately see that it has *intentions*, but more background knowledge is required to see *what* its intentions are. The consciousness of an elephant, dog or cat, is no more 'hidden' from you than is anyone else's consciousness. The consciousness is there, right before your eyes, manifested in the animal's body. It is a misunderstanding to search for consciousness in the brain alone.

Consciousness is the centre of my body and my world. We cannot locate the ego by pointing at it, but if we were to give it a location anyway, we would have to say that the ego is simply in the body as a whole. Kant emphasizes this in his early work *Dreams of a Spirit-seer*, where he says that were we to attempt to say *where* the soul is, we would have to say: 'Where I sense, *I* am. I am as immediately in my fingertips as in my head . . . my soul is wholly in the whole of my body as well as wholly in each of its parts.'[10] To be conscious is to be present in the world, with a body as an agent. Consciousness is visible, but you also have the ability to see it. On the other hand, it is visible in a different way from how, for example, a rock or chair is visible. Consciousness is visible, but it has to be understood. We may say that it is visible because it can be understood.

We humans are vertebrates with large brains; we come up with ideas and are quite good problem solvers. The same can be said of a great many other animals. Since we have so much common evolutionary history with these animals, it seems reasonable to attribute to them some of the same qualities that we attribute to people, not least a consciousness. The prerequisite for animals to be understood is that we have sufficient psychological characteristics in common with them so that we can understand them based on our own psychology, even if we must take into account that the differences will be significant. Humans and animals share so many biological, behavioural and relational properties that it would be strange if we did not share a few psychological characteristics as well.

We have five types of criteria that partly overlap and which in their own way give us reason to believe that an organism has consciousness, preferences, intentions and so on: (1) language, (2) behaviour, including non-linguistic communication through use of signs, sound and smell, (3) the ability to learn and solve problems, (4) neurological similarities with humans and (5) evolutionary closeness to humans. All of these criteria have vague boundaries – it is not obvious how we should define language, for example – but they give us reason to assume that different animals have certain abilities. Trees and plants do not meet any of the criteria. Some will argue that trees and plants communicate, or even have their own language, but they are using these words in such a broad sense that there is no reason to attribute consciousness to trees and plants for that reason. Some animals meet only one or two criteria, others most of them. As we have seen, I believe that no animals other than human beings meet the criteria for language. It is not the case that an animal meeting several of the criteria is necessarily 'more conscious' than an animal that meets fewer criteria, because there will also be questions about *how* the animal meets the criteria.

Starfish do not have brains, so there is no great reason to ascribe a consciousness to them. Having said that, it is tempting to do so because to us it may appear as though they have them;

their behaviour is so seemingly deliberate that we would normally have attributed this to having a consciousness. There are also large grey areas, and it is far from clear where we should draw the line between animals with a consciousness and those without one. In 2012 a number of researchers within neuroscience signed a statement called *The Cambridge Declaration on Consciousness*, claiming that a number of non-human animals, including all mammals and birds, and octopuses, have the neurological conditions for consciousness, and that many of these animals display such clear signs of consciousness that the burden of proof now lies with whoever wishes to deny it.

The Australian philosopher Peter Godfrey-Smith uses the giant Pacific octopus as his starting point when arguing that the normal view of consciousness, as something that one either has or does not have, is wrong.[11] Everyone agrees that humans have a consciousness, and most would also argue that chimpanzees and dolphins do too. On the other hand, very few would argue that ants have a consciousness. In between is a vast number of animal species that, to varying degrees, appear to show signs of consciousness. The problem with viewing consciousness as something which comes in degrees is that it is not so easy to imagine what it means to have 'a slight consciousness'. It is one thing to have some degree of memory, but to be 'slightly' conscious of pain is something different. It seems natural for us to say that either you feel pain or you do not. However, Godfrey-Smith points out that if we view consciousness as something which has developed throughout evolutionary history, it is most reasonable to view it as something that has developed little by little, rather than something that did not exist until one day it suddenly appeared complete, in a creature. Consciousness, as we have it, where we can form a kind of inner image of external reality, is presumably a further development of the ability to have subjective experiences. It is not unreasonable to assume that many animals that have no consciousness of the kind we have can experience basic phenomena such as pain, hunger and thirst. Or to experience that one needs air after staying too long under water. These are feelings we experience ourselves having – and with us they are combined with a rich ability to form a more-or-less objective image of the outside world – but it is not unreasonable to think that one can have experiences like this without this ability. We can see that chicken and fish, when injured, choose foods containing painkillers, even if they are not their favourite foods and when their favourite food is available. This indicates that they feel pain and choose food that reduces the pain. How does pain feel to a chicken? It is not easy to say; basically we can do no more than attempt to compare it with our own experience of pain.

However, when we discuss consciousness, it is important to distinguish between different *types* of consciousness. The American philosopher Ned Block distinguishes between what he calls *phenomenal consciousness* and *access consciousness*.[12] Access consciousness means that an organism has mental states which can affect or be affected by other mental states and behaviours. Imagine placing your hand on a warm hotplate and immediately pulling away. It happens so fast that you are not really conscious that you are conscious of the pain. We can then say that the pain is part of your access consciousness because it causes a behaviour, withdrawing your hand, despite the fact that you do not yet have a conscious experience of the pain. After that your attention can be directed towards the pain, so that you *experience* the pain. Then the pain is a part of your phenomenal consciousness. Phenomenal consciousness means what it is like for an organism to be precisely that organism, how the organism experiences the state it is in, which in this case is a state of pain.

To have access consciousness, but not phenomenal consciousness, can be highlighted by a medical case where a woman referred to only as 'DF' suffered brain damage from carbon monoxide poisoning.[13] More specifically, she lost the ability to see an object's shape and position – all she could see were extremely vague spots of colour. If you asked DF to describe the room she was in, what objects were there and how they were placed, she would be unable to. However, she would be able to walk through the room without bumping into a single obstacle. If you asked her to push a letter into a narrow slot, she would have no problem, even when the slot was adjusted to different angles, but she had no experience of seeing the crack. Her access consciousness worked fine – sensory impressions came in and caused the desired behaviour – but she had no experience of these sensory impressions.

To complicate things further, we distinguish between first-order and higher-order theories of phenomenal consciousness. First-order theories argue that phenomenal consciousness

consists of having a type of perception of oneself and one's surroundings. These perceptions are probably widespread in the
animal kingdom, perhaps right down to the level of insects.
The question is whether theories like this capture what is meant
by phenomenal consciousness. Supporters of the higher-order
theories think not. They require that these states must be states
that the organism is 'aware of', which in one way or another are
registered subjectively and *felt* in a particular way. This is probably
a more reasonable interpretation of phenomenal consciousness,
but in that case it would mean that phenomenal consciousness
is a much rarer phenomenon in the animal kingdom.

The very same behaviour – such as protecting a damaged
body part – can be explained both by assuming that the organism has only access consciousness and by assuming that it also
has phenomenal consciousness. In isolation, this behaviour itself
does not provide any basis for deciding which explanation is the
correct one. As for animals related to us, we can also use neurological findings as a guide by starting from the neural basis for
phenomenal consciousness recognized in humans, and from
that we can see if we find similarities in other animals. It gives us
reason to assume that quite a few animal species, and all mammals
at least, have phenomenal consciousness. What about animals
not so closely related to us? It is doubtful that any invertebrates
other than certain octopus species have it, and after all nearly
98 per cent of all species are invertebrates. For example, we have
little reason to assume that crustaceans have a higher-order phenomenal consciousness because they do not have the neurological

capacity we normally assume one must have for this consciousness to be possible. At the same time, there is reason to believe that crabs feel pain, for example, since crabs have pain receptors and a behaviour that indicates they are trying to avoid whatever is causing the pain.[14] In other words, they seem to have access consciousness, but not necessarily phenomenal consciousness. So they feel pain, but have no *awareness* of feeling it. What that feels like is hard for us to imagine, because our pain awareness is so steeped in phenomenal consciousness, but the example of the warm hotplate perhaps give us an indication. However, we also know from human experience that the affective dimension of pain – that it is troubling – is distinguishable from it being noticed. There are people with particular brain injuries who have reported noticing pain, but also that it does not trouble them.

Nevertheless, as a rule of thumb we should say that if an animal behaves in a way similar to a human in situations where we know that humans feel pain, we should assume that the animal also feels pain – and that it bothers them – unless we have good reasons to believe that the animal does not have the neurological prerequisites for experiencing pain. This type of behaviour is not found in insects. They carry on as normal with their activities, as far as is physically possible after injury – for example, they will continue to eat even if half the body is cut off and the food just flows out again – so judging by this, pain does not exist for them. But it does for us, and for many other animals.

SIX

Intelligence

A problem when determining whether, or how, animals think is that we are so undecided about what we mean by 'thinking'. Our concept of thinking stems from human life, and even that must be considered vague; but what is sufficiently clear is that we are able to use it in daily language without noticeable misunderstandings. If you were to ask me: 'What are you thinking?' I would not wonder what you meant by the expression 'thinking'. It is more problematic when we use the expression about an animal's mental activity. If I say that a crayfish cannot think, it is unclear what I am saying. The question is: precisely *what* is it that I claim it cannot do? Of course, a crayfish cannot solve even the simplest mathematical task such as: 'What is 7 + 5?' Nor can it read and write. Is possession of these skills the same as thinking? These activities are examples of thinking, but humans without these abilities would still be credited with an ability to think. So-called 'wolf children' are an example of this.[1] One well-known case is the so-called 'Wild Boy of Aveyron', who on 9 January 1800 emerged from the woods of Saint-Sernin, France. He was about twelve years old, could not speak, relieved himself while standing upright and without warning, and tore off his clothes if someone dressed him. Victor, as the boy was eventually called, also frequently bit those who came too close. His relationships with the people around him were no more than vehicles for fulfilling his primary needs. Victor was a primitive human, yet most people would be inclined to say he was thinking. We must then ask ourselves, with regards to expressing thought, was there any fundamental difference between Victor and the animals he had grown up with in the forest? There does not seem to be. So we have taken this concept of thinking into the animal kingdom, but how far should we go? That clams cannot think is quite uncontroversial. However, it is highly likely that all mammals can – along with all bird species and a few octopus. The basis for this claim is that they have the ability to solve problems and to vary their behaviour according to the circumstances. Clams cannot do this. The diversity in between these groups is enormous, and it is more than doubtful that we will ever be able to draw a clear line through the animal kingdom between the thinking and the non-thinking. So we must be content with a vague line, if that is the best we have.

There is overwhelmingly good reason to claim that many animals think, at least mammals and a number of other species, but there is also good reason to claim they do not have language. This also goes for the few highly trained individuals – such as Washoe the chimpanzee and Koko the gorilla – who have a particular ability to use signs. As already mentioned, I doubt that it is reasonable to ascribe to them the ability for language, as we would normally understand language. My point is more that a great deal of thought takes place, within the animal kingdom, outside the class of humans. The thinking takes place without language as a medium; in some form of non-linguistic medium. It is hard for us to know what kind of medium this should be, but we can imagine, for example, that it is a form of mental picture.

When we watch chimpanzees looking for a solution to a problem, one that is principally about food, it can appear as though they are pondering. As already mentioned, we do not know *how* they think, but it would be close to assume that they see objects in their imagination – which they can deconstruct and reassemble, move around and compare – in a multidimensional, inner space, almost like a film, perhaps. We may never decide exactly how to test such a hypothesis, so we will just settle for saying that it is conceivable that it is like that. The content of these images or films may not necessarily be translated into normal verbal language. Most people would agree that a painting can contain things that cannot be expressed in normal language; and in the same way the mental content of animal minds cannot be directly translated into normal language. We humans also possess this kind of non-linguistic dimension of thinking, and it is therefore possible that we can share an animal's non-linguistic thoughts. In that case, language is not 'a universal medium for understanding', as the German philosopher Hans-Georg Gadamer and others have claimed.[2] Having said that, it must be given that human comprehension essentially takes place through language. If intelligence should be understood as the ability to solve problems, there is no obvious reason that it would require an ability for language. On the contrary, we find this ability for problem solving in a variety of species to which we have no reason to attribute language.

It is difficult to evaluate the intelligence of different animals compared with each other for the simple reason that it is not clear what standard one should use to evaluate intelligence. Whatever is 'intelligent' must presumably be considered relative to the environment of the individual organism, and animals live in very different environments. In basic terms, the problem is that there are no neutral standards. In the absence of any standard, we have nothing but comparative assessments, and these assessments require certain frameworks better adapted to the behaviour of some animals than to others. There is not one indisputable correct standard for intelligence, and different animals can only be considered more, or less, intelligent depending on the standard used. We can always compare two species based on their ability to solve a particular type of task and find that one species performs much better than the other. However, the ability to solve that particular type of task is not a neutral standard. It might be more central to the life of one species than to another.

We have no other standard for intelligence than the human one, and anything more or less intelligent has to be referred to according to this standard. Quite how this standard should be formed is another matter – it's not certain, for example, that IQ is a suitable measurement. Human intelligence has many dimensions, too, from the ability to solve mathematical tasks to carrying out practical matters. The point is, nevertheless, that our concept of intelligence stems from human mental life – it is from there that we have acquired this idea of what it is to be intelligent. Some may then claim that 'intelligence' means something totally different when we talk about species other than humans, and they must be allowed to say that; but at the same time it should be pointed out that they do not know what they are talking about, since they too have no other concept of intelligence than the one drawn from our consciousness.

In order to judge an animal's intelligence, the normal approach in science has been to give the animals practical tasks with varying degrees of difficulty, to see to what extent the animal is able to solve the task without human help. However, this procedure is not without problems. For example, wolves usually fare better than dogs in these tests, but it's not certain if wolves are more intelligent than dogs. The wolves try to solve the tasks on their own, while the dogs turn far more to people for help. Getting someone else to solve a practical problem for you is also a form of intelligence. In general, I'm inclined to say that my pets have been better at training me than I have at training them. Of course, I have trained them to a certain extent, to make them house-trained and so on, but they have trained me to organize my existence around their needs, to check if they are hungry, need a trip, or want food, affection or for me to decorate my home so that it suits them. So perhaps intelligence should therefore be measured pragmatically, by seeing if the animal's behaviour – whether it is independent or gets help – leads to the practical outcome the animal wants.

One animal that became famous for its intelligence was a horse named Clever Hans.[3] He appears in literature as a constantly recurring example of how we allow ourselves be fooled into believing that animals have far more refined mental skills than they have the capacity for. Clever Hans was given credit for solving various tasks, including arithmetic, reading and spelling, that were incredibly advanced. For example, he managed to answer questions like 'What is 7 + 5?' and 'If the ninth day of the month is a Wednesday, what date will Saturday be?' He could also answer questions that were written down on a note he was given. The owner of Clever Hans, Wilhelm von Osten, was a maths teacher and horse trainer. Since the horse eventually became so famous, German education authorities established a review commission with thirteen presumably competent members, and in 1904 the commission concluded that there was no deception involved in Clever Hans's sensational feats. However, the psychologist Oskar Pfungst investigated the matter further a few years later, attempting to carry out a more controlled test. It turned out that Clever Hans was able to give the correct answer when someone other than his owner asked the questions, but it also turned out that he was able to answer correctly only when his owner knew the answer. After closer examination it was clear that the horse responded to small movements which his owner had no idea he was making himself. When Clever Hans stamped twelve times with his hoof after being asked 'What is 7 + 5?', it was not because he could actually add, but because he was able to register the small unconscious movements made by his owner.

It would have been not only impressive, but hugely surprising, if a horse had the ability to solve mathematical tasks like '7 + 5 = 12', for the simple reason that a horse's life and interests are not concerned with those things. One lesson we can draw from the example of Clever Hans is how important it is to carry out controlled tests whenever possible, but something rarely pointed out is just how impressive what this horse actually did was: he was able to interpret his owner's tiny unconscious movements and translate them into stamping his hooves, and that in itself demonstrates a not insignificant level of intelligence.

Pigeons, with a little training, can to some extent distinguish between Bach and Stravinsky, although they are not terribly good at it.[4] On the other hand, they are amazingly good at distinguishing between the paintings of Picasso and Monet.[5] Not only that: when pigeons were presented with paintings by Braque, Matisse, Cézanne and Renoir, they placed the Braque and Matisse paintings with Picasso, while they placed the Cézanne and Renoir paintings with Monet. From an art-history perspective it was an excellent choice, there are plenty of human museum-goers with a worse eye for visual art. However, we haven't the slightest idea of exactly *what* the pigeons see in the paintings that allows them to make this differentiation between painters. Does this differentiation mean that the pigeons have the ability to form concepts? It depends on what's required in order to say that someone has a concept. Humans can undoubtedly sort objects without actually having a concept of these objects. For example, you can have a person sort out parts from discarded computers, and teach them to place all the circuit boards in one pile, without the person being said to have a concept of what a circuit board is. On the other hand, one can say that the person actually *has* a concept of circuit boards, but it is primitive and consists of the following characteristics: 'Flat cards that are usually green and with a thin layer of copper strips that go to different parts of the card.' This is a concept of a circuit board that contains no understanding of how these cards function in a computer, but it is nevertheless a concept of a circuit board.

If such an ability to differentiate is sufficient in order to have concepts, it is reasonable to ascribe to pigeons the ability to form concepts, even though we have no idea what it is about these concepts that makes it possible to differentiate between the various painters. If this ability to differentiate is sufficient in order to have concepts, it must also mean that language is not a necessary condition for having concepts, since similar abilities for differentiating can be observed in a variety of animals that do not have language.

The ability to learn is an indication of intelligence, and learning occurs largely through imitation, which is widespread in the animal kingdom. We find it not only in humans and other primates, but in animals with fairly limited cognitive abilities, such as insects. It's an excellent evolutionary strategy because the individuals one imitates often have characteristics that are beneficial. Individuals with a less beneficial behaviour will be imitated to a lesser extent, for the simple reason that they die earlier. One can imitate a fear response, for example, although there are also inherited fear responses. One example of an imitated fear response is the rhesus monkey's fear of snakes. This fear occurs only in monkeys that have grown up in the wild, not those that have grown up in captivity. The explanation for this is that wild monkeys learn this fear response by imitating the behaviour of other frightened monkeys. We also find imitation based on the observations of a variety of species outside the mammal world. A well-documented example of a learned behaviour is the blue tit, which has learned to open milk bottles. It was first observed in a small village on the south coast of England where a blue tit pecked a hole in a milk-bottle top and gained access to the nutritious milk. Afterwards, the locals began to see this happening with an increasing number of milk bottles, and over the following decades, the practice spread across the whole of Britain and even to Europe.

Humans teach each other all sorts of things. Learning occurs in many other species, too, not least because younger individuals mimic those with more experience; but an individual taking on the role of teacher for another is more rare. An example of this might be a mother dog teaching her puppy to walk down the stairs by going down first and showing how it's done, then walking up the stairs again and going down with the puppy. A clearer example is where adult meerkats teach young meerkats how to kill scorpions, and seem to adjust the difficulty level according to the age of the student; so they try first with scorpions that are easier to cope with, because the sting has been removed or something similar, and then they will take on increasingly demanding opponents.[6] Thus the teacher-student relationship is not limited to humans, but again the huge variation between all that humans teach and learn is striking.

Meerkats have only one thing on the curriculum: killing scorpions. There are also other species that get a similar 'schooling'. Domestic cats bring live birds and rodents to their kittens so they can practise on them. Killer whales teach their young, step by step, how to slide onto the beach to catch seals, and how to get back into the water again. Dolphins release live fish they have caught so their young can practise catching them. There are probably more examples, but we're talking about a relatively rare phenomenon, and it must be underscored that the cats, killer whales and dolphins only have one subject at school. With language as a medium, humans can teach and learn with far greater breadth, speed and precision.

So animals other than us humans can form perceptions of the world based on their experiences. Some animals also have an ability to reason, to draw conclusions from the experiences they have had. However, we human beings are alone in asking the question: 'Is the evidence for belief X sufficient in order to have reason to believe that X is true?' Nevertheless it must be acknowledged that humans, bafflingly often, do not ask themselves precisely that question, and also maintain their beliefs even when there is basically little to support the beliefs and a great deal going against them. Humans at least have the ability to ask this question – unlike animals. So we should also ask ourselves this question when we consider whether animals can think or acknowledge themselves.

SEVEN

For Now We See through a Mirror, Darkly

In Paul's First Epistle to the Corinthians (13:12) it says: 'For now we see through a glass [or mirror], darkly.' It should be said that the mirrors in Paul's time were polished metal surfaces that gave a far less accurate reflection than today's mirrors do, but what we see in our crystal-clear mirrors can be anything but clear to us. Who actually is the person staring back at me from the surface? I don't have a particularly good grip on this character. This relation to myself, when I try to understand myself, is linguistically mediated. So language is necessary not only for communicating my thoughts to others, but for communicating them to myself. As Kant writes: 'We need words, not only to understand others, but also to understand ourselves.'[1] We do not always succeed, but nevertheless we would never have been mysteries to ourselves without language. For most of us, it is likely that this mystery will never be completely solved during our time on Earth. However, one thing is clear to me, and that is that it is *me* I see in the mirror.

The mirror test for self-recognition was created by American psychologist Gordon Gallup in the 1970s and involves applying a coloured mark to the foreheads of various individuals without them being aware of it, and then placing them in front of a mirror. It was believed that if an organism has the ability for self-awareness, it would recognize itself in the mirror and, consequently, understand that it has a mark on its forehead. It would then appear to examine the spot and possibly attempt to wipe the coloured mark off. Humans are able to pass the test, from the age of eighteen months. Many chimpanzees and orang-utans have also passed it. However, the majority of chimpanzees and orang-utans do not.[2] It should also be noted that many chimpanzees that pass the mirror test on one occasion fail it later.[3] After the age of fifteen, a chimpanzee's ability to pass the mirror test decreases significantly without us knowing why. Whether gorillas, elephants, dolphins, killer whales, magpies or pigeons have passed it is a matter of dispute. Another problem with the mirror test is that chimpanzees, for example, touch their foreheads quite frequently. In an experiment testing how often chimpanzees with a dot on the forehead touched their forehead when they were *not* in front of a mirror, they observed a slightly lower touch rate than with the mirror, but not that much.[4] In that respect we can easily end up with false positive results in a mirror test. A bigger problem is perhaps the likelihood of false negative results. We cannot say that animals that fail the mirror test lack self-awareness. The test itself can be so alien to them that the mirror does not interest them enough to catch their attention. Or there may be species-specific reasons for them not looking into the mirror. For example, gorillas, who prefer to avoid eye contact, are extremely reluctant to stare into another pair of eyes in a mirror.

Cats and dogs are nowhere near being able to pass the mirror test. For dogs this is perhaps not so strange. Dogs are first and foremost guided by smell, then sound, and thirdly by sight. Since a mirror has no smell, the dog has no great reason to be interested in it. When young dogs look into mirrors, they will sometimes behave as if they see another dog, but they lose interest once they realize there is no smell. Older dogs do not normally care about mirrors. On the other hand, in the area of smell, they can distinguish between themselves and others. When I'm out with my dog, she barely shows any interest in the areas she has marked herself, whereas areas marked by other dogs are hugely interesting. The dog can easily manage to distinguish between herself and everything else. She has never confused her own leg with a bone. A dog chasing its own tail will tend to stop quite quickly when it realizes that it is part of its own body. If adult dogs chase their tails, it is often a sign that things are not as they should be.

What about human children? Do they pass the mirror test? As mentioned already, they do not normally pass the test until they are aged eighteen months. However, there are large cultural differences. In one study, children from Kenya, Fiji, Grenada, St Lucia, Peru, the USA and Canada were compared. During play, a sticker was secretly placed on the forehead of children aged between three and five, who were then allowed to look at themselves in a mirror for thirty seconds. The result was that 84 per cent of children in the United States and Canada removed the sticker. Should we then conclude that the remaining 16 per cent of these children lacked self-awareness? Not at all. The results of the other countries were clearly weaker: St Lucia (58 per cent), Grenada (52 per cent), Peru (51 per cent) Kenya (1 per cent) and Fiji (0 per cent). Should we therefore conclude that only half of the children in St Lucia, Grenada and Peru have self-awareness, and that children in Kenya and Fiji are simply devoid of self-awareness? Absolutely not. It actually tells us that culture, surroundings and experience play a decisive role in how to handle this sort of test.[5] Furthermore, we know that there are adult humans who clearly have self-awareness, yet do not recognize their own face in a mirror. In the most serious cases of those suffering from prosopagnosia, patients not only lack the ability to recognize the faces of family and friends but are unable to even recognize their own face. All in all, I'm inclined to say that the mirror test is quite worthless as 'proof' of whether a person or a species has self-awareness or not.

What these animals that pass the mirror test show is that they are able to grasp that there is a connection between the mirror image and their own body, and that is no small matter. In any case it's a bit odd to consider the mirror test as a proof of self-awareness. When you look at me, you see my body, and when you look into a mirror, you see your own body. That body can show *signs* of awareness, but self-awareness is not a *thing* that can be observed. If it was, we would be able to answer questions like: how wide is awareness? How tall? What does it weigh? And perhaps: what colour is it? The absurdity of these questions clearly shows us that awareness is not a material object.

For Immanuel Kant, self-consciousness, reason and language are what makes the crucial distinction between man and animal.[6] He certainly believes that animals have concepts, that they find their way in the world, and that they change their behaviour in accordance with these concepts.[7] Viewing animals like mere vending machines, as we find with Descartes, is something he thoroughly rejects. Having said that, he believed that animals have no capacity for self-consciousness, no ability for introspection, and their consciousness is limited to a consciousness of the world beyond themselves. An animal's behaviour can be caused by internal conditions such as pain or hunger, he believes, but it cannot make this pain or hunger into an object of its consciousness.

The human self, as Kierkegaard puts it, is a relation that relates to itself.[8] We also relate to other selves that relate to us. We have an ability to think about what others think and feel about us, and how we are considered by others means something to us. It is not clear if any other creature than man has this self, as in a relationship that relates to itself. The animal is a mystery to us, but not to itself.

EIGHT

Time

In letter 124 to Lucilius, the Roman philosopher Seneca writes that animals live in an eternal *now*, inextricably linked to what is available to their senses in the present.[1] A horse can recognize a road, he claims, when it is on the road itself, but it has no recollection of the road when it is in the stable. The past is present only when the horse is reminded of it by something in the present, and the future is never present, he claims. This is a widespread perception when philosophers write about animals.

Similarly, the French philosopher Henri Bergson writes that a dog that recognizes his owner, and shows this by wagging its tail and barking, does not do so by eliciting a picture of the past.[2] The reason for this is that the dog lives completely in the present, and only humans have the ability to free themselves from the present, he claims. One question that arises is: how he can be so sure of this? It is well documented that animals have memory, sometimes an amazing memory, which in some respects goes beyond the human one. Chimpanzees, for example, are able to remember numbers that surpass those we humans are capable of.[3] Of course, we are talking about chimpanzees that have received training in this, but they outperform humans who have also received this training. In an experiment where numbers from one to nine are shown on a screen in random order, and where those numbers must then be typed in the same order afterwards, chimps need far less exposure to each number than people do. They are also able to remember the running order in a deck of cards to a greater extent than human memory experts are capable of. They seem to have photographic memory and great mental capacity. We cannot say exactly how the past makes itself apparent to an animal's consciousness, whether it is through pictures or otherwise, but that the past *does* make itself apparent seems indisputable.

That many animals also have some kind of concept of the future is evident from them being able to predict the behaviour both of their own species and of other animals. There are various explanations for how they are able to do this; some theories assume that they are able to understand what is happening in the consciousness of other animals, while other theories simply claim that the animals have learned that a certain type of behaviour is usually followed by another type of behaviour. Personally I am more inclined to go with the latter explanation. Either way, it is clear that animals anticipate events. They can expect something to happen, and can express disappointment when it doesn't. Every dog owner has seen their dog become immensely happy when they put their shoes on – because it could mean they are going for a walk – and that similarly the dog becomes dejected when you walk out the door without them. Conversely, the dog may become dejected when you put your shoes on because it can mean you are going out without them, and then become filled with pleasure when you grab its lead. They can also retain past experiences in their consciousness. Without any previous experience of someone grabbing the lead, suggesting that you will be going for a walk, the animal would not have the expectation of going for a walk when the lead is picked up. So the animal's experiences contain more than is actually provided to the senses there and then, and the animal draws from previous experiences and anticipates future ones.

A fascinating example of systematic planning for the future is Santino, a male chimpanzee at Furuvik Park in Sweden.[4] Like so many other chimpanzees in captivity, Santino had an acute dislike of the zoo's visitors. It is not unusual for captive chimpanzees to throw objects, usually excrement, at them. Santino, however, was far more thorough with his planning than most chimpanzees: early in the day, before visitors arrived, he would walk around gathering stones, which he left in piles. When the visitors arrived later, he bombarded them with this ammunition. An interesting feature is that he was quite calm when he collected the stones and furious when he threw them. After a while, he expanded the normal stone ammunition to using concrete lumps he had broken off from his enclosure. This wasn't quite what the zoo wanted, so they went round removing the rocks he had gathered before the visitors arrived. Santino's way round this was to build different hiding places from straw and conceal the stones there. When Santino displayed aggression, and the guides began ushering the visitors away from him and out of his throwing range, his response was to pretend to be a truly peaceful chimpanzee and approach the visitors in a friendly manner, only to then explode and bombard them with stones as soon as they were within range. You have to admire Santino's determination. In the end, the zoo chose to castrate Santino to reduce his hormone levels and make him more peaceful, and the result was a more playful, slightly rotund chimpanzee. The question is how we should understand Santino's behaviour. What is going on in his consciousness during this process? That he makes plans for the future is clear when, by collecting stones, he does something which is not beneficial to his present self, only his future. This behaviour is also found in other species, for example collecting nuts for the winter. However, Santino shows such great flexibility in his behaviour, by making such large changes in his approach towards reaching the goal, that it is almost unavoidable to regard it as a determined thought process relating to concepts of future behaviour.

Dogs and other animals can remember past events and people they have been linked to, but *how* the past makes itself apparent in a dog's mental life is another matter. Can a dog picture events from the past in his mind? It is impossible to say, since we cannot, as already mentioned, see inside the dog's inner life and observe what is going on there. However, we can observe that dogs have what appear to be dreams, where they whine and growl and move. The same applies to cats. In tests, where the mechanism in the brain that prevents movement during REM sleep was disabled, the sleeping cats lifted their heads as if they saw things; they fought, and crept up on prey.[5] It is easy to interpret this as an external sign of an internal mental state. However, we do not know how they dream. Since cats are so guided by their sense of vision, it is easy to think it is in the form of pictures. Given how strongly a dog's sensory experience is associated with its sense of smell, it is not unthinkable that they smell when they dream. And bats: is their dream life most associated with hearing? We know that electric eels also dream, but how do they dream? If animals have mental representations or concepts in their dream life, as we have, it is not unthinkable that they too can have mental representations of their past when they are awake. But there are many *ifs* here. So what *kind* of concepts they might have is also quite open.

It is obvious that animals can remember where they have previously found food. Not only that: they also seem to remember what they can find, and where, so we are then talking about quite advanced mental operations. Birds have this ability, for example. In one experiment, scrub jays were given worms and peanuts which they could hide.[6] A significant difference between worms and peanuts is that the worms decompose quickly and become inedible while the peanuts can remain edible for a long time. However, these birds have a clear preference for worms over peanuts. When the birds searched for food a few hours after they had hidden it, they first picked their favourite food, the worms, and then the peanuts. Five days later, however, the situation was quite different: the scrub jays did not even bother looking for the worms, which had become inedible, and went straight to the places where they had hidden the peanuts. This indicates partly some form of understanding of the shelf life of different types of food, and partly remembering what is where. Based on these experiments we have good reason to ascribe a reasonably good memory to the birds, but for that reason we do not know much about what it is like for the scrub jays to have this memory – for example, whether its consciousness of what it remembers is in the form of mental images.

We also do not know *how* animals experience the past and the future. But one thing we do know is that different animals experience time differently. For we humans, 24 still images per second – as used in regular analogue movies – creates an impression of one continuous movement. For a pigeon, however, it will look like a series of still images, since it updates its visual impressions at a much higher frequency than we do. Dogs also have a higher frequency than humans, but a lower one than birds. This is another important reason why my dog has never managed to catch a bird, no matter how hard she has tried. The birds simply update the visual information much faster than she does, which gives them a head start. At the opposite end of the scale we find snails that are only able to separate events from each other if more than a quarter of a second passes between them. If you wave a stick in front of a snail four times a second or more, it will see just one motionless stick.

Man's capacity for language gives time a different role in our lives than in the animals. We have no reason to assume that animals other than ourselves *dwell* on the past, and nobody other than ourselves are so hooked on nostalgia from another time. It's highly unlikely my dog lies deep in thought about how cosy we had it in the cabin one weekend last autumn in the warmth from the fireplace with a storm raging outside the cabin walls. Nor does she lie there looking forward to the next cabin trip, or make plans to unearth a nice bone that she hid a few metres from the cabin. We humans, on the other hand, live to a large extent in the past and the future, and it is by drawing from the past and the future – who we have been and who we are to become – that we fill the present with meaning. The past clearly remains valid to the life of animals, such as when a dog recognizes its owner after being separated for a long time.

A well-known literary example of this is Odysseus' reunion with his dog Argos after being away for twenty years travelling – first for ten years in the Trojan War and then ten years journeying home to Ithaca.[7] In Odysseus' absence, several suitors have taken over his house and have wooed his wife Penelope. Odysseus wants to return home in secret to confront the suitors, so he disguises himself as a beggar. As he nears home, he sees the dog Argos lying abandoned in a heap of animal excrement, flea-ridden and reduced to a shadow of the strong dog he had left. Unlike everyone else, including an old friend, Argos immediately recognizes Odysseus, lowering his ears and wagging his tail, but is too weak to get up to meet his old owner. Odysseus cannot comfort the dog either, as it would reveal his identity, so he walks by as a tear drops from his eye, and then Argos dies.

NINE

Can Animals Be Understood?

The philosophical tradition devoted to explaining what characterizes human understanding of the world, hermeneutics, is generally uninterested in animals. Most of the hermeneutical descriptions of animals – if they mention animals at all – testify to having very little experience with, and even less of an understanding of, animals. In fact most of them claim that animals cannot be understood, only explained.

The distinction between understanding and explaining originates specifically from the German philosopher Wilhelm Dilthey (1833–1911). He claims that we *explain* nature and *understand* the soul, and that the former belongs to the natural sciences, while the human sciences deal with the latter.[1] The object of the human sciences, the spirit, is not only presented as something internal. It is also given an *external expression*, as when someone expresses something with words or gestures, plays an instrument or applies paint to a canvas. Dilthey describes this as the spirit *objectifying* itself. These external expressions differ from what we observe when we look at raw natural phenomena because they are signs of an inner life. According to Dilthey, the objects of the natural sciences are 'mute' because they do not address us, while the objects of the human sciences are meaningful. Human actions and statements have meaning while a chemical reaction or hurricane does not. However, Dilthey's distinction becomes problematic when we talk about animals rather than rocks or trees because animals actually have an expressive life. Animals express feelin gs like joy, anger, love, sadness and so on, as does so much of the art we appreciate. Of course, we must acknowledge that there is a difference between the expressions of humans and other animals, but it does not prevent us from finding external expressions of an inner life in animals as well. One would then think that this can be made into an object for understanding, not just for explaining.

Understanding, according to Dilthey, consists of a *re-experiencing* of someone else's mindset, and when it is particularly intense, he calls it a *re-feeling*. A *re-experience* will always have to be based on external signs that are interpreted as signs of an inner life. Many assumptions must be made about the sender in order to understand him or her, to actually have any understanding that there is anything at all to be understood. You must assume that the sender is actually expressing something. After that, you need to understand what conventions form the basis of the expression – for example, you must know that a particular gesture means this and that in a given context. Then you must have knowledge of the situation in which the expression occurs. All this means that you need to have understood a great deal before you can begin to understand anything. As Dilthey sees it, we can understand other people because we have the same 'being' as them. Therefore, because we do not have the same 'being' as the animals, we cannot understand them. An animal's expression of life is therefore not an object for interpretation.

For Dilthey, understanding always has an emotional dimension and he therefore emphasizes that the interpreter must have 'sympathy' for the object. But this sympathy does not extend further than other humans. We can say that this is where Dilthey's argument falls apart, because he simply assumes that there is nothing to understand in an animal's mental life. Dilthey had studied Darwin's texts and was very familiar with the principle of adaptation. However, he believed that there was a crucial difference between the adaptation of humans and animals: in that, by adapting, humans gained a form of control over both their own instincts and their external nature, while animals can do nothing but follow their instincts. An animal lacks a centre for its consciousness and is therefore wholly at the mercy of external circumstances. Unlike humans, an animal can never create its own life story or express any subjective opinion. Dilthey claims that he is leading the way in interpreting life itself, and that life experience expresses itself as signs. But it is only human life and human signs that he sees. Elsewhere, he writes that 'the structure and articulation of life exists everywhere where there are inner, psychological phenomena, consequently in the entire animal- and human world', but he does not follow up on this.[2]

Hans-Georg Gadamer had the same attitude as Dilthey, and it is striking that the word 'animal' is not found in the comprehensive index to his main work *Truth and Method* (1960). For Gadamer, animals are to be considered simply as natural phenomena, and all natural phenomena should be considered solely as effects of causes. It is unacceptable to view an animal's behaviour as an expression of experiences or as a subjective presence in the world. Only a being with a language can express subjective experiences. As he sees it, only that which has language has any world at all. Paradoxically, animals do not have a relationship with the world because they are too fully immersed in the world. He writes: 'Having a language means exactly having a way of being that is completely different from how animals are bound to their surroundings.'[3] Language creates a distance from the world, and therefore makes a relationship with it possible. Language can present something to us, even when it is not presented to the senses. The animal is subject to its circumstances, while humans can orientate themselves in the world. An animal's relationship with the world can be boiled down to the world being a source of satisfaction of its subjective needs, while human beings can guide themselves towards an objective reality.

There is a somewhat greater openness for making animals into subjects for understanding by Gadamer's mentor Martin Heidegger, even though he claims that there is an 'abyss' between animals and humans.[4] He believes that we come close to an understanding of the animal's experience of the world through an analogy based on our own experiences and empirical knowledge of the animals. In a series of lectures from 1929 to 1930, Heidegger distinguishes between stones, animals and humans by saying that the stone is world-less, the animal is poor-in-world and humans are world-forming.[5]

As Heidegger sees it, animals have access to things. They can sense things and relate to them, something a stone cannot do. Therefore, the animal has a world while the stone does not. However, in contrast to humans, animals do not have access to things 'as such' because they lack an 'as-structure' in the experience.[6] All recognition is a recognition of something *as* something. 'As' is the relationship between 'something' and 'something'. The original relationship to things is a pragmatic relationship, where they are not experienced as mere things, but as things that are *for* something – that is, objects for use.[7] Heidegger claims that this use of things is a condition for being able to pass judgement: 'This is a hammer.' The use of the hammer precedes talking about it. In *Being and Time* (1927) Heidegger claims that speech is not a fundamental aspect of our existence, but instead has its roots in an understanding of the world that precedes talking about it.[8] Language is therefore the articulation of our understanding – more specifically, an understanding that is already there before it is expressed linguistically. For Heidegger, each human action is always already an interpretation. When I get up in the morning and put on my slippers before collecting the newspaper, I am using the slippers *as* tools to prevent my feet from getting cold or wet. After reading the newspaper, I will shuffle into the bathroom to take a shower, and then take off the slippers, because they are impractical to wear when you shower. These actions and my relationship with the slippers are *interpretations*. The reason they are interpretations is that in both cases I have considered something *as* something. This 'as something' is essential to the interpretation.[9] At the same time, this is a criticism of the notion that every interpretation includes language, because I do not need to have said, or thought, a single word while performing several of these actions. As Heidegger points out, one cannot conclude that there is a lack of interpretation on the basis of there being a lack of words.[10]

Heidegger will claim that a dog can smell a leaf lying on the ground, but the dog can never experience the leaf *as* a leaf – something that fell from a tree, and that the fact that it fell from the tree indicates that a new season is on the way. The dog does not see something *as* something, but exists in a continuum with the outside world. The animal is poor-in-world because it is totally immersed in the world. My dog lies by the fireplace warming itself, but it does not relate to the fireplace *as* a fireplace. It can never distance itself from the fireplace and recognize what makes the fireplace a fireplace, Heidegger would say. Animals will always be 'trapped' by things because they are in an immediate relationship with them.

The dog, however, sees the couch *as* something it can lie on, the ball *as* something it can play with and the steak on the countertop *as* something it can eat. The dog does not reflect on the 'being' of the couch, or the ball or the steak, but it relates interpretatively to its surroundings and, in the process, with a form of as-structure. Also, it must be acknowledged that very few people devote much of their attention to pondering over the couch, the ball or the steak's 'being'. With regard to being 'trapped' by things, many animals have an ability to change their behaviour when their surroundings change, such as a human when a tool no longer works. For a long time, it was believed that only humans have this capacity for adaptive behaviour, but as Donald Griffin and others have shown, even that which appears to be routine behaviour in animals varies depending on the situation.[11] Flexibility is important because it is an indicator of consciousness. To the extent that we can give a clear answer to why consciousness arose in some species, it is because it enabled organisms to vary their behaviour according to the circumstances.

A number of animals seem to fulfil these descriptions of having an interpretive relationship with the world based on an as-structure. However, the animals lack language, and Heidegger seems to say that language is always implicitly there in activities that are seemingly language-free.[12] Throughout his writing, language becomes increasingly central to Heidegger's philosophy, and the more strongly he emphasizes this – so that 'language is the house of being' – the greater the distance between humans and animals.[13] Among other things, he writes that the animal is closed off from language, and that language is man's most significant ability.[14] Man creates a world because of its language. I agree with Heidegger that our language forms a crucial distinction between us and all other animals, but this does not mean that animals have no understanding and interpretive relationship with the world that we can attempt to understand. This perspective, however, is of very little interest to Heidegger, and besides his lectures of 1929–30, he makes few attempts to penetrate the animal world. More precisely, the animal for him during the rest of his authorship has only the negative role of helping to define man, by being something that does not match a human because it lacks language.

For Heidegger, because animals are essentially not in an interpretative relationship with the world, there is not much to understand in an animal's life. However, there are elements of his philosophy that, in my opinion, may be useful in our attempt to understand animal life. This applies, for example, to his concept of 'disposedness' (*Befindtlichkeit*). With the term 'disposedness' Heidegger wants to describe what it is like to *be* in the world.[15] One could say it is a response to the question of how we are. To be in the world is to experience the world as a place containing objects that are both meaningful and uninteresting.

This disposedness has a fundamentally emotional quality. It is the emotions that allow certain objects to be perceived as meaningful and that, strictly speaking, allow for participation in the world. It is disposedness, for example, that enables something to be perceived as threatening. For Heidegger, emotions are not purely subjective, but rather 'the fundamental way that we are outside ourselves.'[16] If we can say that an animal's presence in the world has such an emotional, subjective dimension that it *is* in one way or another, for instance, frightened or excited, then that would be the animal's disposedness. There is good reason to attribute this dimension to the animal's life, and then it should also be possible to make this into an object for understanding.

The German philosopher Max Scheler elevates what he calls 'sympathy' to a form of understanding he presents as an alternative to the objectifying view in the Cartesian tradition.[17] As Scheler sees it, the researcher should, with the help of his imagination, attempt to reconstruct the reality of the subject he has set out to understand, rather than reduce it to a mere object. We should do this when we try to understand not only people, but animals, he claims. We will then be in a position to embrace the *whole* animal kingdom with our understanding and sympathy. We understand and feel it when we see an animal that is in pain or afraid. However, we must develop our sympathetic, intellectual capacity for understanding animals. We can understand them by being aware of the behavioural and expressive signs that refer to their mental state. All animals have a 'grammar of expressivity' which we can learn to understand, but this understanding demands that we apply both our intellectual and our emotional abilities.

It is *joy* we are witnessing when two elephants meet again after having been away from each other: where they twirl around and flap their ears while making a distinctive rumbling noise as a way of saying hello. Or what about two reunited chimpanzees who hug each other, stroke each other's backs and occasionally kiss? Obviously we cannot feel exactly what is going on in the elephant or chimpanzee's emotional life, but we can imagine these feelings based on how it is be reunited with someone who means a lot to us.

When I hear the sound of birds who have located the bird-feeder I've hung out for them in the cold, I hear the sound of frenzied contentment. I believe they think it is good. The dog, lying next to me by the fireplace, lets out a few grumbling sounds which I can only interpret as a sign she is extremely comfortable. Animals that have the ability to feel have the ability to feel pleasure, and they seek to achieve this pleasure just as we do. In order to grasp this pleasure, you basically need no more than your experience, imagination, empathy – and to observe the animal. But without using your own feelings, you will never be able to understand the animal's feelings.

TEN

Surroundings

D o we live in the same reality as animals? The German-Estonian biologist Jakob von Uexküll (1864–1944) introduced the concept of *Umwelt*, a self-centred world, to the study of animals.[1] This term is difficult to translate into English. It literally means the world that surrounds an organism, and it could be described as the world as experienced from the perspective of that specific organism. Uexküll stressed that all organisms have *their* self-centred world, which differs from those of other organisms. We can say that the 'self-centred world' describes an organism's subjective reality. Imagine you are walking your dog, and that your dog has a flea in its fur. You then have three vastly different organisms, which are, objectively speaking, located in the same environment; but they have three different self-centred worlds because they relate to the different parts of this environment in different ways. We could perhaps say that an environment can accommodate an infinite number of different, experienceable worlds. Uexküll compared the self-centred world to soap bubbles in which every single organism is trapped. Different organisms can have widely different sensory organs: some have incredibly sharp eyesight while others have no eyes at all; some can see ultraviolet light and others are colour-blind; some have especially good hearing while others have an excellent sense of smell. Most animals have a sense of smell, but mammals of the Cetacea order, such as whales and dolphins, are an exception. Dolphins cannot smell, despite having a form of nose. The location of their sensory organs plays an important role, too. The human field of vision is approximately 200 degrees, while a pigeon's field of vision is 340 degrees. So it is clear that humans take in their environment in a way that differs widely from pigeons, because we mostly take in whatever is right in front of us, while a pigeon can take in almost everything around it – obviously this provides a quite different experience of being in that space. On the other hand, pigeons have lousy depth of vision, while ours is excellent. Animals will often live in different parts of the environment, too: some in the air, others in the trees, many on the ground, and others under the ground or in the water. One can say that each organism has its own section of reality to which it relates, and this section is the organism's self-centred world.

Meaning is attributed to the world by the beings that live and act within it. The world in itself is meaningless, and there is no neutral meaning in the world either because different beings, with different self-centred worlds, will always project their own meaning onto it. Nor will there be one self-centred world for all people: if a hunter, a lumberjack and a botanist enter a forest, they will have three quite different self-centred worlds because the forest will be defined by so many different characteristics. Self-centred worlds are defined by a range of 'carriers of significance', which are strongly linked to the organs the animal uses for sensing and interacting. Primitive organisms will perhaps have only a few carriers of significance. The tick for example, has only three: (1) the smell of butyric acid, which is excreted in a mammal's sweat, (2) the temperature of 37 degrees Celsius, that of a mammal's blood, and (3) a sense for skin which is not entirely covered by fur. The surroundings of a dog or cat, on the other hand, will have a high number of meaning bearers.

All things in an organism's self-centred world are defined by their function, but what function they have varies from organism to organism. An object without function does not really exist in the animal's world, and the very same object can have widely different meanings in different self-centred worlds. Uexküll gives an example of a dog which is trained to jump up onto a chair and sit there when it hears the command 'chair'. If one removes the chair and gives the dog the same command, the dog jumps onto something else, a couch or a table, and sits down on that. These things are defined by their function for the dog: they are something you can sit on. Much of what has an obvious function for us humans, like a fork or a clock, will be meaningless to a dog. If a clock is ticking loudly a dog might notice it, but most likely the ticking will simply blend in with the background noise of the dog's surroundings. To a dog, a pen is not a writing tool, but perhaps a stick you can chew on. It's quite amazing how much of a dog's self-centred world actually falls into the 'something to chew on' category.

Animals are *interpreters*. They form their own self-centred worlds. Animals that create good interpretations survive, while animals that create bad interpretations do not. Survival is, as such, the criterion for an interpretation's appropriateness. Animals are *subjects*. Being a subject is synonymous with being at the centre of a world. Experience of the world will therefore always be a subjective experience. There is not one book of nature, but just as many books as there are organisms. Or at least just as many as there are species. The question which arises then is: how do we understand the self-centred worlds of other organisms? Uexküll will not go so far as saying that an animal's world is totally closed to us, claiming that an animal's behaviour will show us something about its self-centred world, but we have no other access to the world of an animal than that. Uexküll's depictions of the surroundings of those species most different to ourselves – such as sea urchins, ticks and jellyfish – are described as excursions into unrecognizable worlds.

Dolphins, octopuses and bats have a sensory apparatus that differs significantly from that of humans, and will therefore essentially take in different aspects of reality from those we do. All experience, including that of humans, is partial or limited. When we recognize certain aspects of reality, we obscure others. This does not prevent us from being said to have an objective recognition of reality as it is, but we have no total recognition of it. For example, take the psychologist Joseph Jastrow's famous drawing which depicts both a rabbit and a duck.

We have to say that this drawing shows a duck because people who know what a duck is will be able to identify this as a drawing of a duck. The same goes for the rabbit. Anyone who knows

Joseph Jastrow's drawing, from *Fliegende Blätter*, XCVII/2465
(23 October 1892).

what a rabbit is will be able to see that this as a drawing of a
rabbit. To recognize the drawing as a rabbit and duck, respectively, is objective. However, it is impossible for us to recognize
the drawing as a rabbit and a duck *at the same time.* We are only
able to acknowledge certain aspects of the drawing at a time.
Furthermore, we might also think that the drawing represents a
number of other objects but, due to our own limitations, we are
unable to recognize them.

Certain parts of reality will always be out of your reach
because they are outside the area your senses can take in. Some
of these limitations can be overcome by technology: like using a
heat-sensitive camera to view infrared radiation, which provides
access to a sensory modality found in certain snakes, fish and mos-
quitoes, but not normally you. However, we can also imagine that

there are many other sensory modalities in existence of which we are completely unaware. Animals with different sensory modalities to us will relate to a different reality – or, more precisely, a different fragment of reality – from ours. Most cat owners have wondered how their cat can sit staring at an empty wall, but it's not certain that it really is staring at an *empty* wall. Perhaps there is something infinitely fascinating on the wall that is simply not accessible to the owner's senses. As Montaigne writes:

> The first consideration I have upon the subject of the senses is that I make a doubt whether or no man be furnished with all natural senses. I see several animals who live an entire and perfect life, some without sight, others without hearing; who knows whether to us also one, two, three, or many other senses may not be wanting? For if any one be wanting, our examination cannot discover the defect. 'Tis the privilege of the senses to be the utmost limit of our discovery; there is nothing beyond them that can assist us in exploration, not so much as one sense in the discovery of another.[2]

It is basically impossible for us to decide whether animals have completely different senses, as Montaigne suggests. It is therefore not a particularly fruitful hypothesis, since it can be neither confirmed nor rejected, but it is quite conceivably so. What we can say for sure is that many animals can perceive phenomena with their senses that we are unable to with ours. For example, many animal species can sense imminent earthquakes or electrical storms. On the other hand, humans have developed technologies that can uncover these things even earlier than animals. Friedrich Nietzsche expresses the point clearly in an essay from 1873:

> It is even a difficult thing for him [the human] to admit to himself that the insect or the bird perceives an entirely different world from the one that man does, and that the question of which of these perceptions of the world is the more correct one is quite meaningless, for this would have to have been decided previously in accordance with the criterion of the correct perception, which means, in accordance with a criterion which is not available.[3]

In Plato's dialogue *Theaetetus*, Socrates quotes the so-called *Homo mensura* doctrine of the sophist Protagoras: 'Man is the measure of all things: of things which are, that they are, and of things which are not, that they are not.'[4] Socrates believes such relativism to be untenable, that there should be no standard for what exists and is true, irrespective of the human perception of the matter. Among other things, he tries to refute this position by saying that one should then also say that even a pig or a baboon is the measure of all things.[5] This point of view, however, is not as absurd as Socrates assumes. There are many measures. Man is the measure of all things – but only for man.

ELEVEN

To Be an Animal

We humans can try to grasp another organism's self-centred world. In which case we should not only use anthropomorphism. We should also make some attempt to put ourselves in the animal's place through *theriomorphism*, where instead of giving animals human characteristics, we do the opposite: we give humans animal characteristics. You can try to be the animal that you have set out to understand, be it a dog or cat or an octopus. In this attempt to become the animal, to move like one and sense the world from the animal's perspective, you will gain a greater understanding. A wonderful example of this strategy can be found in *Being a Beast* (2016), by the British veterinarian, barrister and philosopher Charles Foster – an eccentric book, to put it mildly.[1] It begins with Foster wanting to know what it's like to be a wild animal, and the book is a sometimes insanely funny description of how he, among other things, attempted to live like a badger, on a Welsh hillside, for six weeks. He also tries to live like an otter, a fox and several other animals. There is a lot of nudity and freezing. He eats insects, worms and roadkill. Several of the animals he tries to become are animals he likes, whereas he detests otters. Of course he fails to become a wild animal – a person can never be a badger or an otter – but he fails in an excellent way. You can try to get close to a dog's surroundings yourself by wearing glasses that impair your vision a little and walk around on all fours sniffing the ground. If you really were up for the task, you should also eat other dogs' excrement, since that is a real delicacy for most dogs, but it is way beyond the limits of what most of us are willing to do to learn how to better understand a dog's life.

Even if you were to go in for the task wholeheartedly, it will still only give you a very limited insight into what it's like to be a dog. In an influential article from 1974, the American philosopher Thomas Nagel posed the question: 'what is it like to be a bat?'[2] According to Nagel, neuroscience can never bring us closer to understanding what it's like to be a bat, and the same goes for all other external observations. Nothing about our knowledge of a bat's brain can tell us what it is *like* to orientate oneself using echolocation, or to fly. No matter how much knowledge we collect from a third-person perspective, it will never give us a first-person perspective. This objective knowledge will not be able to tell us what it's *like* to have an experience, such as drinking beer, for example. One can give a physical description of the beer as it runs into my mouth, the signals from the nerve fibres, the beer's journey down to my stomach and so on, but this is not the same as describing the qualitative experience of tasting beer. Beer causes chemical changes in the tastebuds that send electrical impulses to the brain. When I sense the *taste* of beer, a qualitatively new element has come into play. No matter how precisely we examined the brain, nowhere would we find a place where we could observe the taste of beer. The experience of taste is not available for observation in the same way that the brain's processes are. The same applies to sensations like pain, and it will also apply to what it is like to orientate yourself by echolocation, or to fly.

Nagel has a point, but his point is not quite as good as he thinks, and his examples are not so well chosen. As far as the experience of flying is concerned, we have hang gliding, para-gliding and not least wing-suits that can provide us with an experience of flying, because we do actually fly when we use this equipment as a flight prosthetic, an extension of the body. One can assume, with good reason, that flying is quite different for a bat – which has this as a part of its normal condition – than for a human, who is not equipped for it naturally, but one will never-theless have an experience of flying. So what about echolocation? Here Nagel fails, since this is an ability we humans actually do have. At the most elementary level, echolocation is in use when you hear the buzz of a mosquito and, based on the sound alone, conclude that it is located just to the right of you, roughly in line with the back of your head. Sailors have used echolocation – by shouting and listening to the echo – in thick fog or pitch darkness to determine how close they are to the shoreline. Blind humans can develop a remarkable ability for echolocation. By closing our eyes or walking in darkness while making clicking sounds, we can get some idea of how this works. You would normally be capable of determining whether you are in a small or large room, for instance. We have a capacity for echolocation, but it is normally underdeveloped in humans because we usually let our eyes do most of the work.

We could also imagine developing a tool for making our capacity for echolocation just as good as the bat's. However, this would not provide me with the experience of being a bat, just an experience of being a human with a sensory apparatus resembling the bat's. The subjective experience of being a bat, to the extent that a bat has this experience, will always be beyond our reach. Nagel is right about that. But you could say it's a fairly trivial point, consisting of no more than an indication that your consciousness and a bat's are not exactly the same. One consciousness cannot just wander into another, to see it from within so to speak. The consciousness of another is essentially *another* consciousness. This not only applies to our relationship with animals of a different species, but to our relationship with other humans. There are also other experiences that I have no access to. I could ask questions like: 'what is it like to have perfect pitch?' or 'what is it like to experience synaesthesia?'

Nevertheless, it is clear that we can draw on our first-person experiences in our attempt to understand what it is like to be a bat. By sharpening our own echolocation skills we can claim that we have at least come *closer* to an understanding of what it's like to be a bat. We can use our imagination, our own experiences and knowledge of the animal's physiology and behaviour to get closer to such an understanding. The overlap between the lives of other animals and ours is significant. If we limit ourselves to the mammal group, we have things in common such as a reproductive system that produces live young which need to be taken care of. There are great similarities in the need for water, food, sleep and, not least, air. One can stimulate the same parts of an animal's and a human's brain electrically, and provoke the same emotional response. We find similar behavioural deviations in humans and animals with corresponding abnormalities in their brains, such as compulsive behaviour. Humans and animals respond similarly to many medicines, and develop addictions to many of the same substances. It should also be acknowledged that the mammal class is heterogeneous, to put it mildly; the smallest species weigh only a few grams and the largest weigh up to 160 tonnes and these species live very different lives. All other mammals can nevertheless still experience pleasure, sadness, fear, anger, surprise and disgust.[3] This gives us a comprehensive emotional repertoire in common. These feelings will differ in humans and other animals. We could say that an animal's feelings are less polished than ours – they appear unfiltered. However, they are highly recognizable. The neurophysiology of fear is similar in rats and humans: the amygdala – the brain's emotional centre – is activated and sends out signals to the hypothalamus and pituitary gland; adrenaline and cortisol are released in large amounts, the nervous system quickens, and the pupils dilate. Fear works differently in the lives of rats and humans because we fear such different things, but it is common to us on a basic level – this is precisely why we can recognize it in animals. This is probably the most fundamental part of understanding animals: being able to recognize their feelings. And, second, understanding why they feel what they are feeling.

In a similar way to humans, I consider an animal's feelings as cognitive instruments. Theories on feelings will normally emphasize the following traits: feelings are *subjective* phenomena that have *valence*, or meaning; they are positive or negative, not neutral. A feeling has an *intentional object* – it is *about* something. Often, feelings are of relatively *short duration*, and the duration is determined by a change in the valence.[4] Emotions can be viewed not only as purely subjective events, but as cognitive instruments, meaning they contribute to telling us something about reality. Feelings, like all other instruments that we use to acknowledge reality, can give us a correct or incorrect picture of reality – for example, about what poses a real danger to us. Since emotions are also cognitive instruments, to understand an animal's feelings is also to partly understand the animal's experience of the world, and that means to share the animal's subjectivity and its self-centred world.

We can only see behaviour, but this behaviour can be loaded with meaning, and this meaning is something we grasp almost immediately when we interact with humans or animals we know well. Look at the behaviour of a dog, cat or chimpanzee mother that takes care of its offspring – its behaviour is loaded with meaning that testifies to it having a strong inner life, and it is immediately understandable. At other times, like when we deal with people from a culture other than ours, we can immediately *see* that there is meaning in their behaviour, although it can be difficult to grasp exactly *what* that meaning is. Rituals within religious practices that are not familiar to us are a clear example.

It is necessary to acquire an intimate knowledge of what you want to understand. This also applies when understanding animals. The understanding of animals requires that you interact with animals. A dog that 'bows' is expressing a clear intention to play – it is a kind of invitation to play, and is immediately understood by other dogs, as well as people who have learned to interpret this behaviour.

If we are to understand other people, we must presuppose what is commonly called the principle of charity. This means we have to view those we are to understand as fairly rational, or more precisely, that they have perceptions of the world that are reasonably close to our own. Without making this assumption – where we view whatever it is we hope to understand as more-or-less similar to us – the understanding process cannot begin. If I meet a person who speaks a language that I have never heard before, and he points to a glass of water while saying what sounds to me like 'usjabig!', I ought to assume that 'usjabig' means 'water', 'glass', 'drink' or something similar. I need not assume that the person suffers from hallucinations and is saying 'fire-breathing dragon'. Of course we cannot be sure that 'usjabig' means 'water', 'glass' or 'drink', but I will find out eventually. Either way, I have to start by assuming that he has ideas about the world, and a behaviour, that also makes sense from my perspective.

The same applies when we set out to understand animals. When my dog, who has not received food that morning, stands at its food bowl looking at me pleadingly, I should assume it is hungry and wants food. It turns to look at me, and it wants a response, and in this case it is most reasonable to assume that the desired response is that the food bowl is filled up. When I'm working in the office at home, absorbed by my writing, I might sometimes feel a damp, cold nose nudging my lower back. It normally happens at times where we would have gone for a walk, which makes it easy to interpret this as an expression of a desire or need to go for a walk. If we are to understand animals, we must begin with what we have in common with them. When we understand animals, we enter the animal's world.

TWELVE

The Dog

It is normally claimed that the dog became domesticated about 14,000 years ago, based on the discovery of dogs buried alongside humans, but some of these archaeological findings also indicate that this process – where dogs were taken into our homes – occurred as many as 36,000 years ago.[1] The dogs we now have as pets develop later than the wolves they are akin with; they open their eyes later, and are also older before they begin walking or play-fighting. Compared to wolves, it is tempting to say that our dogs never grow up and, more precisely, remain at a full-grown puppy stage throughout their lives. What this 'puppy' fills your life with is, at the very least, joy. The happiness that radiates from a dog, as it runs after a ball and catches it, indicates pure *joy* at being in the world. Every dog owner has experienced the pleasure of being met by such huge excitement when walking in the front door. My dog is no exception. Luna shows how happy she is by wagging her tail, jumping, sniffing and barking jubilantly. After this initial greeting, she'll usually run to get her favourite toy, make squeaking sounds with it and then show it to me. Similarly, we know how dejected dogs can become at the sight of a suitcase, when their ears droop and their tail does the same.

When a dog looks into its owner's eyes, a large dose of oxytocin is released into the dog's brain. Oxytocin is a crucial part of the biochemical basis for having a sense of attachment to others. For the record: dog owners also receive a good dose of oxytocin in the brain when they look into their dog's eyes. Dogs get a greater increase in oxytocin levels than cats get from looking into their owner's eyes. However, the differences between species vary somewhat. I have had cats that have behaved quite similarly to dogs and I have had cats that have behaved more like cats, and I have liked the former best. I have also had dogs that have behaved like cats and dogs that have behaved like dogs, and I have preferred the former there, too.

Luna has a long nose while mine is short. The inside of a human nose contains about 6 million receptor cells, while a dog's nose has hundreds of millions, up to a billion where some breeds are concerned. They also use a much larger part of their brain capacity than we do when processing all this smell information; and as far as one can tell, they can form complex notions about objects, places and events using their sense of smell alone. From the dog's perspective, your identity is primarily determined by how you smell, and secondly by the way you look and sound. That is why the dog is so eager to smell you, and preferably lick your face, when you arrive home.

Dogs are nearsighted, but at close range, their noses and mouths tell them just about everything they are interested in knowing. Their colour vision is not much to brag about. They are not colour-blind, but they cannot see red, and can generally only see colours in the range between blue and green. They also seem to prefer some colours to others, to a small degree. They can see the difference between a large and a small bowl of food, and prefer the large one, but they cannot see much of a difference between a bowl containing five treats and one that only has four. Dogs are not concerned by what a thing *is* but by what they can *do* with the thing, which will largely concern whether it can be sat on, lain on, chewed or eaten. Things that move interest them more than things that stand still. A dog has only, to a small extent, a preference for things that have one form rather than another – what's crucial is whether the thing fits in its mouth or not. There is almost no limit to what Luna finds edible, although a banana is among the few things in the 'inedible' category. Bones rank highly in the category of things that are edible. However, if I make dog biscuits for her, it is of no consequence whether they are shaped like a banana or a bone.

I often marvel at how bad my dog's vision is. When we are walking along the city streets, and there is a person coming towards us with a stroller, Luna will clearly indicate that she thinks there is a dog approaching whom she is looking forward to greeting. Even I, someone who wears glasses, can see this is obviously not the case. We have to get quite close before she realizes that it is not a dog, and loses interest in what has appeared in her field of vision. As mentioned, she uses her sense of smell for most of her recognition. If any other members of the household have come home before we return from our walk, I will see it in her reaction the moment we enter the lobby of the apartment block;

she will lunge towards this wonderful scent in typical form, eager to get up the stairs to our apartment on the third floor. With each step along the hallway and up the stairs, the smell gets a little stronger for her, so she knows that they have gone that way and are now where the scent trail ends. It doesn't seem so unreasonable to attribute to her some kind of belief that Siri or Iben, my wife and daughter, have returned home. On these occasions, even I am not able to detect any smell indicating that Siri has returned home from work or Iben from school. Perhaps I would have if I really concentrated. We humans, after all, have a far better sense of smell than we usually assume.

Admittedly, we are a long way from the level of a dog, especially when it comes to faraway smells, like the subtle traces of a human who has passed through a city where there are so many other smells; but when it comes to scents within close range, our sense of smell is not at all badly equipped. The main reason smell plays a role that is so much smaller in human life than in a dog's is that, due to our upright gait, our noses are far from the ground – where so many smells are located. We humans could orientate ourselves more in our surroundings using our sense of smell, as dogs do, but then we would have to get down on all fours and press our noses to the ground.

A dog lives first and foremost in the now, but precisely because it is so orientated by its sense of smell, it is a *drawn-out* now. Smells linger in the air, and a dog can distinguish between a new, fresh smell and an old, stale one. A stronger smell indicates something that has happened more recently, while a weaker one suggests it is from longer ago. A smell that becomes gradually weaker as you walk tells you that you are walking away from its source, and in doing so the smell gives you a whiff of the past. Conversely, a smell that gets stronger will tell you something about the future, about what you will encounter if you continue walking towards its source. When I get home from work, Siri asks me how my day has been. My dog does not ask, but sniffs me, and those sniffs tell it everything worth knowing: where I've been, which people or animals I've had contact with, and not least what I've eaten. The sniffs also confirm that it really is *me* entering the door. When the dog meets another dog on the street, they have to smell each other thoroughly, because that's how they sense who the other one is. It is totally unnecessary to *look* at whether the other dog is of the same or opposite sex, because they have smelled it long before they are in a position to see the other dog's rear-end. We humans can, by the way, also make a qualified guess about gender without seeing the dog's rear-end – bitches often sniff at the other dog's face first, while male dogs usually go straight to the opposite end.

Films obtained by attaching a camera to a dog give us a certain impression – a chaotic one admittedly – of the dog's visual perspective of the world. What these films do not provide us with is something far more important to the dog, namely its smell of the world. If you are to even begin approaching a dog's perspective, you must first start by sniffing things repeatedly, and preferably lick them. And not just things but other people, although there is a danger that you might become slightly unpopular. When you start to accumulate knowledge of this kind about your dog, you will begin to understand it – that is, to share the dog's perspective of the world; to understand what it's like to be that dog.

The word 'ontology' originally denoted the philosophical teachings about what essentially exists in the world, but in recent times the word has gained a broader meaning to describe a class of things that different people believe exist. A person's ontology will change throughout life; one will cease to believe that certain things exist and start believing that other things do. For example, as a child I thought that Santa Claus existed, which made Santa Claus part of my ontology, something he is not any more. Most of your ontology remains stable throughout life; for example, you believe there are rocks, chairs, beds, shoes, trousers and houses. An ontology also consists of things that are not physical objects, such as holidays and promises. In short, your ontology consists of everything you relate to as real. We can also talk about an animal's ontology, and that will consist of everything the animal can perceive and have a behaviour towards. In Uexküll's words, an animal's ontology consists of all the things found in its surroundings. Which then makes it clear that my dog's ontology is quite different from mine. Firstly, a dog cannot have anything in its ontology that presupposes language. It can always have things that have names in its ontology, like 'ball' or 'bird', which are the names of some of its toys – and a dog can learn a great many names – but for a dog the existence of these things is not dependent on them having these names. Nor does a dog's ontology contain any abstract phenomena, such as mathematical conditions, laws, money or holidays. Where my ontology consists of a mass of objects that I have never had first-hand experience of, only read about, a dog's ontology only contains objects it has experienced. It is tempting to say that a dog's ontology consists of physical objects such as chairs, sofas, birds and sausages, but then we would only be projecting our own concepts, our own ontology, onto the dog. It would probably be better to sort them roughly according to their function: things to lie on, things to chew on, things to eat, and so on.

Dogs are communicators to a totally different extent to cats. They not only speak to us, but to each other. They also speak to any suspicious characters making a noise outside the front door, telling them to go away immediately. There are sounds that Luna recognizes, like 'Luna', 'Iben', 'Mum', 'stay', 'No', 'walk' and 'food'. Since she would become impatient at the sound of 'walk', I began using circumlocutions like 'trip' and 'air', but she quickly learned to recognize these sounds as well. For the most part, however, my impression is that it is the tone used that is most decisive. The context is also important: if we drive a car and I say the word 'walk', it generates no enthusiasm, nor does it if I am in the shower. It has to be a situation where going for a walk is a real possibility.

The dog world also has its intelligent superstars, who really put Luna in their shadow with their ability to recognize words. For example, a border collie called Chaser learned 1,000 names in the space of three years, and they were all names of her toys. In addition, she learned three verbs, in case the toys needed to be picked up with her mouth or pushed with her nose or her paw respectively. However, it is not clear *what* Chaser has learned. Is it about her having a highly developed ability to associate random sounds with particular objects, which is impressive enough, or does it mean the dog understands that each of these sounds is a *name* for an object? If the latter were true, it would raise things to a completely different level, because it would mean that the dog had an understanding of semantics; but it is unlikely, and it is worth noting that it is still far from what we would normally call a language. What does the dog's own name mean to that dog? Like humans, dogs usually come when their name is called. Cats rarely do this. What does 'Luna' mean for Luna? Does Luna know that she has a name? Hardly. Her name certainly has a role as an important sound, one that normally indicates that something positive will happen. She has at least noticed that she gets a positive response when she comes at the sound of her name.

Luna's communicative register consists of grunting (contentment), whining (self-pity or pain), howling (like whining but worse), howling with joy (usually with someone she is very fond of, but also when playing with other dogs), growling (a rare expression of aggression, but it happens) and, not least, barking. The barking is complex, and cannot be understood independently of the context in which it occurs. She barks to show anger or fear, to warn, express despair, greet, express joy, get attention and so on. If all you hear is a generic 'bark' when a dog barks, you're probably a tiny bit tone-deaf. Barking contains a multitude of meanings.

There are also numerous physical expressions. When she yawns, it's usually not because she's bored, but to calm down others and herself. At the same time, she does sometimes yawn because she is tired. You can also calm a nervous dog by yawning at it. Tail wagging also has its codes. If the tail is held very high, you should watch out. If it is held low while wagging quickly from side to side, it usually indicates that the dog is submissive. Last but not least, we have the 'normal', happy tail wagging that is somewhere between the two. Differences in breed should also be taken into account: some naturally hold their tails high, others low. Dogs also communicate a lot with urine, which tells other dogs who has been there.

Dogs learn from experience, as we do, and they make connections between different phenomena. For example, my dog has learned that the sound of a particular drawer being opened is associated with treats. Luna knows what she likes: food, going for walks and food. And she knows what she dislikes: driving, showering and walking in deep snow. This is evident in her behaviour, where Luna tries to maximize the pleasant things and to minimize the unpleasant. This behaviour is difficult for me to understand without ascribing certain perceptions and preferences to her. I would normally imagine her mental content as being something with the characteristics of a picture. I don't know if she sees pictures, but that's how I imagine that she imagines things. As with other pictures, these mental pictures *hardly* say more than a thousand words, but they do say something *other* than a thousand words, which is precisely why it is so difficult to describe, in words, what this thought-content should specifically be.

Dogs show very little ability to think abstractly. They relate first and foremost to what is immediately provided to their senses. However, it is likely that your dog thinks about you when you are not there, and it may have expectations of something that's going to happen, so it is not completely tied to the present. Dogs cannot think of things they have never sensed, and we have no reason to believe that they can combine different ideas in their imaginations, such as thinking about you wearing a white tuxedo if they have never seen you wearing a white tuxedo. Your dog cannot read your thoughts. In fact, it has no idea that you or itself have thoughts. So your dog cannot trick you or deceive you, since deception and fraud require the perception of someone else's thoughts. Your dog, however, is extremely good at noticing bodily signs, often incredibly subtle signs, and responding to them.

Anyone who has had a dog in the house will have noticed how easily it becomes affected by your mood. If you are happy, your dog will be happy; if you are stressed, your dog will be stressed; and if you are frightened, the dog will be frightened, too. It can also seem as if your dog gets sad when you get sad. Many dog owners claim that their dogs are so good at judging other people, and I have thought this myself; that if my dog shows a real dislike for someone, then it is at least worth approaching that person with a degree of scepticism. Having said that, the dog will often, after a short while, get along amazingly well with the person it was initially sceptical of. Many dogs are generally sceptical of strangers, and Luna is one of them, while others are the opposite. All in all, we shouldn't pay too much attention to the dog's supposed ability to judge someone's personality. Most likely, your dog has noticed something: when you tense your muscles for example, albeit just a tiny bit; or release a small amount of stress hormones that it can smell; hesitate a little, breathe a little quicker or slower, and so on. Dogs have the ability to register these signs – which are so subtle that a human would miss them completely – and translate them, for example, into barking at the person you are uncomfortable about meeting. A friend of mine complained that her dog was 'racist' because it would bark at anyone with dark skin. One can imagine that the dog's barking was caused by the reaction that its owner displayed when meeting people with more pigment in their skin. My friend would, of course, wholeheartedly dispute this, but dogs are, as mentioned earlier, not particularly concerned with what colour anything is.

A dog owner will often claim that their dog knows it has done something wrong because it displays typical 'guilty behaviour': its tail wags quickly from side to side between its legs, its ears turn back and fold flat against its head; the dog will also try to sneak carefully out of the room. It is no small claim to state that a dog knows it has done something wrong, because it implies that dogs too have eaten from the Tree of Knowledge and have learned to separate good from evil. Hardly. If you film a dog that does something 'wrong', you will see no sign of guilt or regret as long as the dog is alone after the 'crime'. It is only when the owner appears that the behaviour starts. So it is most likely that it is the owner's reaction that causes the dog's behaviour, rather than the dog having an awareness that it has done something wrong. This can be confirmed by entering a room where there is a dog that has done nothing wrong and behaving as though it has done something wrong. The dog's reaction will be exactly the same as in the cases where it actually had done something wrong. A dog that has done something wrong does not know it has done something wrong. The only thing it knows is that your dissatisfaction is aimed in its direction, and that it is therefore a good idea to lie low. Nevertheless, my dog has always operated on the principle that it is easier to be forgiven than to get permission. Given how small a dog's frontal lobe is – and we know that the frontal lobe is where the neurological conditions for exercising self-control are – we shouldn't have too high expectations of a dog's self-control; at least not without us being there as an external monitor. It is more reasonable to be pleasantly surprised when they actually do exercise self-control, and not too upset when they don't. Personally I'm impressed with the self-control and ability to understand situations that dogs actually do show, for example when small children pull their tails but are not attacked for it.

Your dog cannot trick or deceive you, if by that we mean expressing something other than what it's really thinking. However, your dog can exhibit behaviours that can be interpreted as such. My dog, like most whippets, is closely related to the princess in the story 'The Princess and the Pea'. She has a very clear preference for making life comfortable, and a very limited tolerance of anything uncomfortable. Some of the things categorized as 'uncomfortable' are rain and cold, and one can agree with her on that. If we go for a walk in the snow or rain, she will start limping and lifting her hind leg. Normally I would then assume that she had pain in her foot, and consequently end the trip quickly so that she can rest. However, it has struck me that she will continue to limp after stopping to do her business, but when starting to walk again she will limp on the other hind leg instead. She has seemingly 'forgotten' which foot was hurting. It is then natural to assume that she is trying to fool me into believing she has a bad foot in order to get home quicker from the terrible weather and curl up in her bed by the fire. However, this would be assuming that the dog is more cunning than it is actually capable of being. It would mean the dog has the ability for so-called 'metacognition', to be able to think about what I am thinking, but we have very little reason to attribute this ability to dogs. A far easier explanation is that the dog has previously noticed a connection between it limping and the walk ending sooner, and as a consequence she now sometimes limps when she wants a shorter walk, without actually giving my thoughts any thought. Perhaps it could simply be that the dog first had pain in one leg and then in another.

Are dogs guardian angels in times of need? Some dogs are. We have all read about dogs that have saved children from drowning, dogs that have alerted others who have come to the owner's rescue, and so on. Dogs for the deaf and blind can perform a variety of tasks to keep their owners away from danger. There are also rescue dogs that do an outstanding job of finding people trapped by avalanches and the like. An animal food brand in America has a Hall of Fame for 'animal heroes' that have performed outstanding feats by saving the lives of other people. Almost all the animals that have received this distinction are dogs, but there are a few cats, too, including the deaf-mute cat Baby, who saved his owner's life by waking his wife, who then saw that he was suffering a heart attack. I don't doubt these stories about how dogs have saved people, but we cannot on that basis say anything generally about what dogs typically do when you or others need help, or about why dogs do what they do. There is an imbalance in which events we get to know about through mass media, and I have never read a news article with the headline: 'Man dies after his dog fails to alert everyone in the vicinity that he had fallen from a stepladder and was unable to move.'

Will a dog help you if you are in need? Most likely not, for the simple reason that it probably would not understand that you are in need. In an experiment to investigate this, two scenarios were created.² In the first scenario, where the owner pretended to have a heart attack, the dog saw its owner grab his chest, gasp for breath and collapse 'unconscious' on the floor. In the second scenario, a bookshelf, made of light materials specially for the experiment, tipped over onto the owner, leaving them pinned to the floor and unable to move while they shouted for help. In both cases there was a person in the room whom the dogs had been introduced to in advance and whom they could turn to. The dogs were then observed for six minutes. What did the dogs do?

Mostly, they went over to their owners and nudged them a little with their nose or leg. Some dogs simply ambled about sniffing the surroundings. Very few dogs made any sound or approached the other person in the room, and only one dog touched this person – this dog jumped onto the person's lap and took a nap. Hardly any of the dogs can be said to have done anything at all to help their owner. The explanation is not that the dogs didn't *want* to help, but rather that they did not *understand* that the owner needed help, because they did not understand what an accident or life-threatening situation is. One thing is missing in the design of the study, and it is scent. Perhaps there would have been a different outcome if the dogs had been able to sense that their owner was secreting stress hormones. In that case, one might imagine that they would smell that their owner needed help. But this is just speculation, and if the owner suddenly fell to the ground without it really noticing, it wouldn't have made any difference anyway.

It may be disheartening for us dog owners to hear this, but you cannot blame a dog because it doesn't understand something it doesn't have the prerequisites to understand. It is like blaming the dog for not being able to solve differential equations. What about situations where dogs *have* helped their owners or others by barking or something similar? It's most likely that the dog found the situation strange or uncomfortable, and handled it as well as it could. There are many credible stories about dogs that have helped people or other animals, and these stories are moving, but they are moving because they are extraordinary. We should not be tempted into believing that they are the rule just because we would like them to be.

To understand a dog, begin with what you and the dog have in common, but if you really are to understand it, you must also be open to everything you do not have in common. A dog is a dog, not a human being, and a dog that is treated far too much like a human by its owners is rarely a happy dog.

THIRTEEN

The Cat

What is it like to be a cat? I have asked myself this question ever since I was little, because the first pet we ever had was a cat. She was called Fia, and came into the house as a stray kitten. After Fia came Fridtjof. Later came the Burmese twins Lasse and Geir. None of them could ever tell me exactly what it was like to be them, using normal verbal language, but they told me a lot anyway by the sounds they made, and their movements. All the years I shared with these cats told me *something* about their experience of the world. Still, one has to admit that it is more demanding to extract information from a cat than from a dog, not least because of the expressionless way cats stare at you – a wide stare that shows no other feeling than the one you choose to project onto it, which makes the cat more of a mystery than the dog. It's presumably why cats are attributed with supernatural powers and insidious plans in so many stories.

It is difficult to train cats in the same way as we train dogs. They learn to eat in one place, and use a tray full of sand as a toilet somewhere else. They can also teach themselves things, like when Geir found out how to open doors, and then continued using that method. One should, however, be entrusted with more than the normal amount of patience if you want to teach a cat to roll around on command, or to fetch a ball that you have thrown. When a cat learns something, it is tempting to say that in many cases it has some representation of a goal. Neither Lasse nor Geir enjoyed being locked in a room, and it was Geir that understood how to solve the problem, namely by jumping up and using his front legs to pull the door handle down. To give a reasonable account of this, we must assume that Geir had preferences, memory, a grasp of the future, an ability to adapt his behaviour, and so on. In short, he needed quite a highly developed consciousness to learn this. He did not have any linguistically structured thoughts, but he perhaps had some form of mental images. We humans have these images, too, like when I now think of Geir jumping up to open a door. Not all of his behaviours were equally sophisticated, but they were expressions of preferences and intentions. Lasse and Geir detested being in the car, and the loud relentless meowing was presumably intended to communicate exactly how terrible they thought it was, so that they could be spared such an ordeal, as was usually the case. It is not unreasonable to ascribe them with communicative intentions.

Lasse was a large cat weighing 8 kg (17½ lb), but he was still less than a tenth of my weight. Geir weighed no more than 5.5 kg (12 lb). Their height was well below my knees, so their view of the world was mostly from a far lower perspective than mine. On other occasions, they would jump onto shelves and other places and view the world from a perspective way above mine. They moved far more vertically than I do. We humans stay more-or-less at three different heights, depending on whether we are lying, sitting or standing, whereas a cat will continually jump up onto things and down from them, and often choose to jump over things instead of walking around them. They are present in the room in a different way from us. A cat's space is more vertically oriented, while a human space is more horizontal. Humans and cats are the same in one important respect: our vision is the dominant sense when we experience the world. In addition to humans and other primates, cats are the only mammals that rely more on vision than on smell. However, cats do not have particularly good colour vision, and they have terrible eyesight at close range, but on the upside they are able to see in almost pitch darkness.

Cats are generally quite inexpressive, and many domestic cats don't make a lot of noise. Like my first cat Fia, who was the *éminence grise* of the house, slipping silently from room to room, and in and out of the windows. Lasse and Geir, on the other hand, were extremely talkative even by Burmese standards and, apart from when they were sleeping, it was rarely quiet. I understood almost nothing of what they said, and suspect there wasn't much there to understand, although the same can often be said of human communication. I thought of it as their small talk, a kind of social glue.

Cats *can* speak, but they speak 'cattish', which is not a language and is something we only partially understand. You eventually learn to distinguish between the different meows, from hungry to anxious to complaining and the one that craves company. For example, the hungry meow rises in tone at the end, while the tone of the anxious one goes down. The hungry meow is repeated in the same way for a while before the emphasis is more on the first sounds of the meow and then increases in volume. It is tempting to transcribe the sound we are left with as: 'I command you to give me some food immediately!' And you then have to concede, because the cat will keep going for longer than you can endure. By the way, giving them vegetables is not an option; the cat is a predator that exclusively eats meat. These variations in meowing are probably something very few cat owners have given much thought to. More precisely, understanding is acquired as so-called tacit knowledge through interaction with a cat. Much of our understanding of animals is tacit knowledge, meaning knowledge that cannot be expressed in the form of statements. Our lives are permeated by this non-articulable, personal knowledge.

You learn to distinguish the self-pitying purring from the normal, satisfied type. There is a different ring to the purring when the cat is sick, injured or dying. But it is for *us* that cats purr. Admittedly, it begins as a form of communication between a mother cat and her young, but adult cats do not purr to each other, only to us. Purring has a frequency of about 25 oscillations per second, within the limit of what the human ear can perceive, and the tone is the same in both sexes, young and old, large and small cats. Apart from when they are in heat – and anyone who has had a female cat can confirm that it is quite a cacophony – and when they are angry, adult cats do not usually 'talk' to each other. The sounds they make are mostly for our human ears. Many cats also make a characteristic hacking sound when they are sitting in the window watching birds outside. We do not know why they make this sound, but a common hypothesis is that it is the cat's attempt to imitate bird sounds, and that it is therefore part of their hunting behaviour. The hypothesis is supported by the fact that larger cats have been observed in the wild imitating the sound of monkeys they are hunting. In addition, there is the loud meowing that some cats make in the middle of the night while we are asleep, which doesn't seem to be aimed at us. But first and foremost cats talk to us humans, and virtually all cat owners talk to their cats. As mentioned, we do not understand much of what cats say, and cats do not understand much of what we say, but there is a form of communication there that goes deeper than semantics. Your cat's communication is something you learn to recognize so well that you know when something is wrong, even when the vet doesn't find anything wrong, and you end up checking the cat even more thoroughly. There are various types of meows and different types of purring, but no cat is able to string them into longer units of meaning, as we humans do when formulating sentences.

Like other cats, Lasse and Geir slept a lot, but they were quite happy to get up before me in the morning. They would want to be fed, of course, and in order to satisfy this need, they would start with a little meowing. Next, it was popular to press my nose repeatedly with their paws. If this did not bring any immediate result then the next step was to lick my smoothly shaved head and, since a cat's tongue is quite rough, my head quickly became sore. If I wanted to sleep a little more, and pulled the duvet over my head, Lasse would jump onto the windowsill beside the bed and make an impressive amount of noise by scraping his paws down the blinds, over and over again, until I would just have to give up on sleeping and get up to feed them. The cats *always* won this fight.

Cats use their meowing to control us, and different house cats develop a repertoire of different meows to get us to feed them or let them go outside. One of Lasse and Geir's favourite things was drinking water from the shower floor, and there was one particular meow that signalled they wanted to do this. It was then just a case of going to the bathroom and turning on the water, while the cats stayed at a safe distance, then turning it off again so that they could drink the water that had collected on the floor. A neighbouring cat wouldn't necessarily have the same meow to signal this need, and even if you understand your own cat's meow, you will not necessarily understand the neighbour's. If I was to ignore their meowing for food because, for example, I wanted to finish reading a chapter in a book while I sat on the couch, Lasse would jump on the TV bench and methodically push DVD after DVD, or book after book, down on the floor while looking at me accusingly.

They had a clear division of roles, where Lasse, who was much bigger than his twin brother, always ate first and was the one who took responsibility for the tough jobs, like waking me up. Geir was a bit more reserved and careful, but a much better technical problem solver. For example, if I shut them out of the bedroom, it would be Geir who opened the door again, by jumping up and grabbing the door handle. I never saw Lasse open a door. Even though they were twins and almost identical in appearance, give or take a few kilograms, they had very different personalities – if one can use that expression about anything other than people – where Lasse was fearless and strong, while Geir was more careful and clever. On the other hand, they were equally social and had a boundless appetite for cuddles. But all the behaviours I have so far described were deliberate and fairly easy to understand.

At other times what is happening in a cat's consciousness is completely incomprehensible, like when it sits and stares into a seemingly empty corner for an hour. No matter how hard I try to see something in the corner, there is nothing there. Or, what really happens in a cat's consciousness when – about once a day, often at around the same time – it seems to go completely crazy and runs from room to room, jumping up on the window-sill, then onto the bookshelves, then down to the floor, onto the bench and down again, as if trying to cover every square metre of the apartment in the minimum amount of time. What is the purpose of this behaviour? I have no idea! Even if we were able to provide a complete physical description of these 'fits', by mapping the cat's brain down to its smallest detail, it's not guaranteed we'd be able to say much about how the experience was for the cat. We can perhaps say something about whether it fills the cat with joy or frustration, since a human brain and a cat brain are also quite similarly constructed, but nothing worth mentioning beyond that.

At the very least, cats bring something of an aesthetic nature to daily life. My dog is slim and muscular, and it can run at an impressive speed: 50 kilometres per hour (31 mph). Watching her run is a pleasure, as she effortlessly puts the metres behind her. It should be said that she doesn't keep this up for many metres because she is a sprinter, not a long-distance runner. Running fast over short distances is an absolute joy for her, while it is troublesome and boring for her to run slowly and for a long time – like when she is jogging with me, for example. However, it is striking how she loses so much of that supreme physical grace when she doesn't run – when she can become quite ungainly. My cats, however, have consistently been elegant. There are occasional mishaps admittedly, especially if a surface is smoother or less stable than the cat expects it will be, but on the whole its physical discipline is almost perfect and it will seemingly – and with great ease – jump from place to place and land, soft as a feather. No less astonishing is how the cat always manages to land on all fours, even if it were to fall backwards through the air. It's an art the cat has already learnt in its second month, and something it perfects throughout life. It appears to do all this so smoothly that it's tempting to describe it as a mere instinct, but it is something the cat has actually learned and then develops further.

There is an old joke about the difference between dogs and cats where the dog thinks: 'My owners keep me warm and dry, they feed me, and give me love and play with me – they must be gods!' The cat, on the other hand, thinks: 'My owners keep me warm and dry, they feed me, give me love and play with me

– I must be a god!' Of course, neither dogs nor cats think this, but it illustrates how we feel the two species relate to us. I have often felt a sense of being admired by my dogs, but this has never been the case with any of my cats. A cat has a sense of entitlement in the world; it takes care of itself and enjoys life as it pleases. It does not worry about yesterday or tomorrow.

Cats are known for their ability to make themselves comfortable. Those that live in the wild rarely spend more than one hour a day on 'work', and even that, hunting, is turned into an entertaining game. They often work on the principle of grabbing whatever chances present themselves, rather than deliberately hunting. In other words, they have a relaxed relationship with work as well. Most domestic cats can, to some extent, manage on their own in the wild. But there are hardly any other pets that can.

To understand a cat is to understand a cat's preferences, which can vary widely from cat to cat. Some flash their tummies to show confidence in you, and others like to have their tummies rubbed. However, one should also be mindful that some cats simply like sleeping in that position, and your hand will get mauled if it comes too close. A cat has an incredible ability to get us to make its life comfortable. It is said that Mohammed, when he was called to prayer one day, took off his robe instead of waking the cat that was sleeping on the lapel. In another version of the story, it is said that he cut off the sleeve of the robe to avoid waking the cat. We really do go out of our way for our pets. In one famous quote, Michel de Montaigne writes: 'When I play with the cat, how do I know that she is not passing time with me rather than I with her?'[1] One cannot be sure of much with regard to an animal so inexpressive as a cat, but the most fair thing to say is that Montaigne and the cat are playing with *each other*. There is some reciprocity there. And just as Montaigne is probably attempting to train the cat, the cat is attempting to train Montaigne. When we live with animals, humans and animals influence each other. However, it must be acknowledged that when you allow a cat into your life, it normally means that the cat trains you more than you do the cat. Cats prefer not to adapt to others, to any notable degree, and it is notoriously difficult to train a cat. We have the expression 'herding cats', which describes the almost impossible task of coordinating or leading many different individuals. The expression is appropriate precisely because cats are extreme individualists and do not follow the pack.

Cats chose us, not the other way round. They moved near human settlements because it was beneficial to them and we allowed them to do it. Dogs, however, were actively domesticated. Human relations with domestic cats probably began in the Middle East more than 10,000 years ago, and since then cats have changed very little. The oldest documented example of a cat buried with a human is 9,500 years old, but we do not know if it was a pet.[2] The oldest visual depiction of cats as pets are found in Egyptian art from around 4,500 years ago. However, cats and humans have a long history, and throughout this history, people have changed more than cats, if not genetically, then in lifestyle. Other animals that have been domesticated by humans have usually changed their appearance along the way, for example their ears began to droop, their canine teeth got smaller and they often gained a more 'childish' appearance. None of this has happened to any large degree with cats.[3] But one major change has occurred, namely a reduction in brain volume of about a third compared to the brains of wild cats, and this reduction is particularly high in areas of the brain related to fear and aggression.

They have evolved in such a way that their natural propensity to be afraid of us has been reduced, and they are therefore more receptive to affection, which is so important to why we like them so much.

One evolutionary advancement the cat has made is that it has a facial shape not totally dissimilar to humans, especially human children. It has a round face with round cheeks, a large forehead, a little nose and, not least, big eyes, positioned at the front in the middle of the face. There is reason to believe that our infatuation with cats is because they look like us, and we therefore tend to project more of ourselves onto them.

It is precisely because cats are not pack animals that their expressive repertoire is so limited. Of course, cats use meowing, purring, brushing up against your legs and flashing their tummies to signal their needs, affection or confidence. There is also hissing, bristling fur, arching of the back and a raised tail that signal the opposite. But cats do not wag their tails to show that they are happy, and they don't flatten their ears unless they are in attack mode. As mentioned, their faces are virtually expressionless. Why would cats have developed a larger expressive repertoire when, throughout their natural history, there has been no pack to show these expressions to?

To stare into the eyes of an unfamiliar cat at close range is not recommended as it is an overly provocative gesture. You should be better acquainted before doing so. However, it can be a good idea to look at it with half-closed eyes and blink slowly – as this creates a nice, relaxed atmosphere. You can communicate with the cat, even if it rarely does as you ask. Cats recognize their owners' voices but, unlike dogs, this recognition seems to raise only moderate interest. Their ear movements suggest that they hear our voices excellently, but they're just not all that bothered about it. Nor do cats seek protection from us to the extent that dogs do. There are great variations between breeds and individuals in terms of how social they are, but in general humans and cats have quite different social needs. For most humans, it is the connection to very few people, the closest ones, which forms the largest part of their meaning in life. Most cats are not like this. It is highly likely that you mean less to your cat than your cat means to you. As a cat owner you might wish that this were different – that you are totally irreplaceable for your cat – but you cannot blame it for being the way it is; it would be like blaming it for not being able to fly, or read philosophy.

There are three times as many pet cats as pet dogs on the planet. This is strange considering how one-sided the relationship between humans and cats actually is: we try to make sure the cat is okay, and the cat does precisely the same thing – it makes sure that it is okay. Cats certainly do not do as we say, and they have no practical use except for catching small rodents, but even in this area the rumours of their effectiveness are quite exaggerated. Dogs can guard, hunt, carry, pull and protect, and they actually do as we say, at least some of the time. So it's no wonder we team up with them. Cats on the other hand . . . It is tempting to describe cat-keeping as the epitome of altruistic behaviour, but it would not be entirely true, because we do get something out of it: we are allowed to share a part of a cat's life, and that is hugely enriching.

Does your cat love you? It depends on the cat, you, and what kind of relationship you have. Most cats do not love you like a dog does, but they will accept you as a central and pleasant part of their existence. You enable the cat to have the life it prefers. Food is always high on the agenda, but as soon as you and the cat have agreed on a routine – which should be adhered to fairly closely to avoid complaints – there is room for mutual affection. But the relationship between the cat and its owner is not purely one of providing food and shelter. If you are travelling, and your cat has a nice cat-sitter that gives it just as much food and affection as you do, it will still appear less content than when you are there. Your cat will be happy to see you, even if it doesn't express it as clearly as a dog. I have had cats who, truth be told, were not in the habit of showing any noticeable joy at me coming home, but I have also had cats that have shown it to the fullest.

FOURTEEN

The Octopus

It is one thing to understand those animals closest to us – mammals like primates, dogs and cats – but what about the animals furthest away from us? An interesting example is the octopus.[1] It is well over 500 million years since humans and octopuses went their separate ways in evolutionary history, at a time when there were no humans or octopuses. By comparison, it is estimated to be 85–100 million years since evolution moved us onto a different path from dogs and cats, and they parted company 30–40 million years ago, while we split from chimpanzees just 6–7 million years ago. We don't quite know what our common ancestor with the octopus looked like, but a reasoned guess is that it was a slightly flat worm, a few millimetres long, with a primitive nervous system and photoreceptors – it may have had some rudimentary eyes.

The distance between the octopus and ourselves is so great, in almost every sense, that it can appear incomprehensible. Let's start with the octopus's body, which is a kind of soft mass, almost shapeless and without bones. Its mouth is in its armpit, where it has a beak. It can squeeze through extremely small openings and has a fondness for escaping from aquariums. The largest Pacific octopus can be 5–6 metres (16½–19¾ ft) in length, and they are enormously strong. Each of the suction cups of an adult is able to lift 13–14 kgs (29–31 lb), and an octopus has 1,500–1,600 of them. While most animals that have a heart make do with just one, an octopus has three, which pump blue-green blood since the oxygen in its blood is bound to copper instead of iron. Their skin is able to create intricate patterns, and they have an astonishing ability to change colour from one moment to the next. The origins of this ability lie partly in its need to become camouflaged, since the body of the octopus is so naked and unprotected; but a colour change can also communicate a state of mind, whether it is in a good or bad mood. There is broad consensus that an octopus is white when relaxed and red when agitated, but beyond it being for that reason, or for camouflage, we barely understand any of the octopus's amazing colour displays. One might suspect that part of this colour display is devoted to communicating with other octopuses, but that is unlikely for the simple reason that octopuses are, after all, colour-blind. The eyes of an octopus have a kind of docile expression; the pupils are a black streak that always lies horizontally, even when its head is leant sideways. They have sharp eyesight due to an advanced eye lens that is not too dissimilar to our own, and it is also likely that they can 'see' with their skin, since it contains photoreceptors. Can you imagine what it is like to 'see' with your skin? To be honest, we don't know much about how these photoreceptors work. They react to light, but we don't know if any information is being sent to its brain. An octopus's experience of its own body must be very different to ours.

What we see when we look at an octopus bears no resemblance to what we see when we look into a mirror. Instead, it's like looking at a creature from an alien planet. Can we understand an animal that is so different to ourselves? Is there anything at all to understand? The answer to the last question seems to confirm this: octopuses display such clear signs of intelligence, and of a rich consciousness, that there is certainly *something* there we would like to understand. The question is whether we are capable of understanding this alien consciousness. When we compare people with monkeys, dogs or rats, there are similarities in our brains that give us a basis for comparison. We can point to the occurrence of certain neural structures in both humans and animals, and when a particular mental ability is linked to a particular neural structure in humans, we at least have a reason to investigate whether the same mental ability can be found in an animal with a similar neural structure. Such a procedure is not possible when we study octopuses. Our large brains are divided into four lobes. The most complex octopus brain can be divided into 75 lobes. Where we can compare the human brain with the brain of other mammals – because the basic architecture is so similar – we do not have this opportunity when we are trying to understand an octopus. The giant Pacific octopus has a mere 500 million neurons, almost as many as a dog and more than a cat. By comparison, we humans have around 200 times more neurons. The number of neurons is a slightly problematic indicator of mental capacity; many bird species have a quite modest number of neurons, to put it mildly, but they are able to solve fairly complex tasks. However, the amount of neurons can at least tell us something about potential. One extraordinary characteristic of the octopus is that over two-thirds of its neurons are in its tentacles, which means that it is highly likely that it 'thinks' largely with its tentacles. Its tentacles even have short-term memory and can continue with their tasks for several hours after being chopped off. What is it like to think with your arms? The location of what we call the brain is also a bit unusual, because it is located around the oesophagus, which is not so fortunate if the octopus eats something sharp.

If you are to understand an octopus, you must first of all look at its behaviour. Octopuses display clear abilities for intelligent behaviour in solving various practical tasks; and they can use tools, but they learn relatively slowly. They are good at finding their way through the mazes that researchers set up for them, and they try to find good solutions for opening boxes with different closing mechanisms. However, it's hard to teach them anything like how to pull a lever to get a reward.

They can recognize people and distinguish between them, even if they are dressed identically. It is most likely that they recognize faces. There are a number of other species that can also do this, not least primates, but this ability has been demonstrated in certain bird species, too, such as crows. Also, an octopus can remember whom it likes or dislikes – if someone has treated them badly, for example – something which, among other things, is demonstrated by a targeted squirting at those they don't like. This is not a one-off thing, but a systematic behaviour. If you stand several people in the same outfit, in front of the aquarium containing the octopus, it will be the person they disliked and sprayed water at earlier who will, once again, get a shower. As mentioned, octopuses have a fondness for escaping from aquariums, and even prefer to wait until no one can see them – for example, when people have left the lab for the day – which indicates that they are aware of whether they are being observed or not. Their behaviour suggests that they can feel pain, since they try to protect the body parts that are damaged, and they also have a well-developed ability to taste and smell. All this makes it reasonable to attribute to them a fairly rich, subjective life.

Octopuses live short lives. Most of them last just one or two years, and even the giant Pacific octopus doesn't live much longer than four years. Both sexes procreate just the once during their lives. Octopuses play. For example, smaller octopuses have been observed carrying two coconut shells which they use for protection by curling up inside them. There is also film of octopuses that curl up inside two coconut shells at the top of a hill and roll down, and then carry the coconut shells back to the top, and roll down again. This is almost identical to what we humans do when sledging. Why do octopuses do it? Maybe because it seems like fun. A broad view on the concept of play is that it is simply a preparation for the serious life that young individuals will have to deal with when they get older. Meaning, this play serves another purpose – that the purpose of the game lies outside the game itself. The problem with an explanation like this is that it does not emphasize the 'aesthetic qualities' of play to a sufficient degree.[2] It is precisely this aesthetic dimension – that it is fun – that defines play. This fun cannot be reduced to something else. There is play that is a preparation for later tasks, but there is also play that is just play. We say that play is *autotelic*, meaning that it is its own purpose. It is this sort of play that octopuses seem to indulge in and it is an indication of what we can call an excess of consciousness.

We can understand *some* of the octopus's consciousness, but not that much. It's quite simply too different to us. Hans-Georg Gadamer describes understanding as a fusion of horizons: a process in which one brings the horizon of what is to be understood increasingly within one's own horizons. This process becomes more demanding the further these horizons are from one another at the start. When understanding animals it is difficult to imagine a horizon further from ours than that of the octopus. We can see if it's relaxed or agitated, happy or angry, that it likes to play but dislikes bright light and captivity, that it likes some people, but not others. But other than that, the inner life of the octopus is largely beyond the reach of our understanding.

FIFTEEN

Loneliness and Grief

C an animals feel lonely? It depends on how you define loneliness. For a long time I believed that animals can be isolated
and under-stimulated, but not lonely. I had to revise this belief
when one of my cats, Lasse, fell ill and eventually had to be put
down. What his twin brother Geir then communicated is difficult
for me to describe without using terms like 'loneliness' and 'sadness'. When Lasse became sick, and his kidneys gradually began
to fail, he stayed away from Geir. They no longer lay together on
the couch, in the basket or under the quilt in the bedroom, as
they always had before – although they did occasionally when
Geir went to find Lasse and Lasse didn't move elsewhere. They
no longer had their daily play-fight, and Lasse no longer cleaned
Geir. When it became clear that no more could be done for Lasse,
a vet came to the house and ended his life with a syringe. Over
the following days, Geir went around the apartment meowing
and looking for Lasse, which wasn't so strange after thirteen years
during which the two had never spent a day apart. But I thought
that it would pass after a short while. I bought pheromone spray
to calm him down, and he received extra helpings of love and
attention. As long as he lay on my lap, he was okay, but when I

had to go and do something else, he continued with the chronic meowing and searching. Things didn't get better over time, which did not heal Geir's wound. It was as though a significant part of the foundation of Geir's existence had collapsed. He was terribly lonely without his brother.

I am not going to claim that I know how loneliness feels for a cat, for the simple reason that I cannot have a cat's mental life. Cats and humans have such different forms of life, and such different cognitive and emotional resources, that a feeling will manifest itself very differently for us. However, we can use what we have in common as a starting point, behaviours which are common to humans and animals, that make some form of communication possible. Lasse and Geir communicated quite clearly to me what they wanted in their daily lives: when they were thirsty and wanted water in the shower, when they wanted food, when they were afraid of something, when they wanted to play and when they wanted love. The question is whether they might also have more complex emotions. I would say that what Geir communicated to me after Lasse died was deep sorrow. How he actually experienced this condition is difficult for me to comment on. I could be accused here of becoming a victim of anthropomorphism in projecting my loss for Lasse onto Geir. On the other hand, as I have said, we cannot essentially avoid using anthropomorphism when we try to understand animals. If we are to understand how an animal experiences something, we cannot avoid using concepts drawn from our own experiences, because our own subjectivity is the only platform we can base ourselves on.

So my response to the question 'can animals be lonely?' is a yes. Social animals can feel social pain, even when the loneliness of an animal and a human manifests itself differently. Studies show that socially isolated parrots die earlier.[1] And we can even observe this in primitive beings such as ants.[2] But we cannot, for that reason, claim that ants experience loneliness. Ants and humans are such different creatures that it is wholly problematic to use a psychological term like 'loneliness', something derived from human experience, for both species. We have a closer and more communicative relationship with cats and dogs. That my dog Luna experiences a social pain that we call loneliness when she is left alone at home, or shut in a room because an allergy sufferer is visiting, seems obvious to me. Her entire demeanour makes it clear. On the other hand, her loneliness is probably very different from the loneliness that affects humans. Human loneliness can be referred to as a divergence of expected and actual attachment to others, but it is doubtful whether we can attribute to Luna a mental capacity like 'an expectation of an attachment to others'.[3] Luna's loneliness is not the same as the one that humans feel. Luna doesn't have thoughts about other dogs playing together, where she is excluded from the game. She has no idea about what kind of connection she should have with her pack. She doesn't have the linguistic and symbolic resources that people have, and this limits her emotional life to what is presented to her there and then. A human's emotional life has a totally different range and complexity because humans inhabit a symbolic universe. Luna's mental life is realized to the fullest in her body.

When with another person, I can wonder about what he or she is 'really' thinking, that in a certain sense there is something potentially fraudulent about the external. In the relationship between two people, there is always a distance because the subjectivity of the other person may also have a hidden element. However, it is not hidden because it is an 'internal' phenomenon, but because the other person conceals it. Nothing is hidden with Luna. So I cannot experience the loneliness in the company of a dog that I can sometimes experience in the company of other people. There is an immediacy in a dog's being that makes a certain type of loneliness impossible. Part of the reason why being with an animal can feel so meaningful is because there is no filter of dissimulation getting between us and them.

However, I'm not sure if Geir's condition should be categorized as 'loneliness'. Perhaps it's more correct to call it grief. Or maybe both. A cat who has lost his closest mate will usually go looking for it, and repeatedly visit the places where they lay together and slept. The smells will fade more and more each day, but the loss remains longer than the smells do. When Lasse died, Geir made sounds I had never heard before. They came from somewhere deep within him. He slept worse and had very little appetite. His behaviour wasn't so different from humans who are grieving. I don't think Geir was grieving that Lasse was dead. He was grieving over the fact that Lasse was *gone*.

The reason he didn't grieve over Lasse being dead was because he has no concept of death. But he missed his brother. How would Geir have reacted if a new cat had come into the household after Lasse had died? It is not easy to say, but after some initial scepticism Geir would probably have welcomed the new cat because he was a friendly soul. It might have eased a little of the loneliness, but I find it hard to imagine his grief being lessened so much that he would have stopped going around looking for Lasse every single one of the not-so-many days he had left himself. Geir was not primarily missing another cat, he was missing *Lasse*. That's what I think. But of course, this is all just speculation.

It must be said that research on the grief process of animals is an underdeveloped field, but we can at least say that when we want to identify the states of grief among animals, we need to look at patterns in their social behaviour, changes in eating and sleeping habits, and other expressions of emotion.[4] These signs vary between species and individuals, as is the case with other emotions. One could contend that an animal's grief must be essentially separate from human grief. And it will be, to the extent that human grief depends on qualities only humans possess. However, human grief is not entirely uniform; different people grieve in different ways. What all grief must have in common is the pain of having lost something unlosable. Human grief differs perhaps most radically from the feelings of other animals in that we can anticipate a loss and start the grieving process *before* we lose someone, because we know it is going to happen; for example, when an illness has a more-or-less inevitable outcome. We humans can also grieve for someone we have never met, like an author or musician we value highly.

It is not easy to decide which animals are conscious of the phenomenon of death. Some animals show clear signs of having an awareness of another's death, such as elephants and chimpanzees. It is more doubtful whether, for example, horses, cows and sheep do. If an animal cannot be conscious of another's death, it is even less likely that it can be conscious of its own death. After all, it is only the death of someone else that we witness, never our own, and this awareness of someone else's death must contribute to an awareness of one's own mortality. It is someone else's death that gives us a concept of death. Frans de Waal wonders if elderly monkeys and elephants have any notions of their own future death.[5] I wouldn't go that far.

However, an animal does not need an understanding of 'death' in order to grieve. It's sufficient that the animal which the other animal is attached to is gone physically, or has become a cold, empty shell. Grieving is due to the awareness of the loss of a *relationship*, and whether or not one has the ability to conceive of this as 'death' or not is less important. In grief, there is a loss so strong that it seems crushing.

Grief does not have to be due to someone's death – it can also be because someone absolutely crucial in one's life has disappeared from it, like a partner who has finished with you. Grief is always about *someone*. It's about losing someone you cannot bear to have lost. Freud writes that both melancholy and grief contain an awareness of a loss, but while the grieving always has a clearly recognized object of loss, the melancholic himself does not quite know what it is he has lost.[6] I doubt that animals can be melancholy but have no doubt they can experience grief.

A well-known example of grieving behaviour in chimpanzees comes from the British primatologist and anthropologist Jane Goodall: following the death of his mother, the male chimpanzee Flint withdrew from the chimpanzee troop. Flint was born when his mother, Flo, was in her forties, which is late. So it is possible that Flo was more nurturing towards Flint than she had been with his older siblings. He was allowed to nuzzle up to her chest and climb onto her back for several years longer than normal. The two were inseparable – until she died. Flint then climbed up a tree, into the nest he and his mother had shared, and refused to eat the food the researchers put out for him. All life seemed to have drained from him, and less than a month later he also died.[7] This kind of grief may not seem advantageous from an evolutionary perspective, and you could therefore question why animals have developed an ability that, instead of advancing, seems to reduce their ability to survive and pass on their genes. The likely explanation is that grief is something which has evolved as the dark side of love. Grief is found in animals and humans because we have the ability to love. Those with the ability to become attached to someone have the ability to feel grief when losing the one they are attached to. One follows the other. To say that animals are able to love is no stretch as I see it.

We regard the animals we live with as individuals, in a similar way to humans. We at least give them their own names, which in itself is an expression of uniqueness, irreplaceableness. My dog,

Luna, is not just any dog, or any whippet. She is *Luna*, and only Luna can be Luna. The same was true of my cats, Lasse and Geir. Lasse was Lasse and Geir was Geir, and no one could take the place of any of them. This specific irreplaceableness is why it is so unbelievably sad when our animals die. I'm not going to say that it's the *same* grief as when I've lost people close to me, because there's a difference between a relationship with a human and one with an animal, but the grief has been deep and I have cried whenever any of my animals have passed away. In that grief there is also something positive – it shows that the relationship I had with the animal was genuine.

Even a dog that you spend every single day with will only have a limited register for communicating with you, and it never learns to relate to the *meaning* of what you say to it. If you are sad about something and talk to your dog about it, you talk *to* it, not *with* it, because unfortunately it doesn't understand what you say, even if it can respond to your mood. When my mother died, my dog looked at me far more than usual; that's how it seemed. Of course, my dog normally looks at me quite a lot, but it was as though she looked extra carefully at me in the period after my mother passed away. It felt natural to me to read a kind of understanding in that look, as if she perceived my sorrow. I also talked a lot to her about the sadness. I knew she didn't understand any of what I said, but it was good to talk to her anyway, just as I talked a lot to my cats after my father died seven years earlier. When I think rationally about it, I don't believe that my dog understood that I was grieving, or that a dog can grasp human grief at all. The dog was probably just reacting to the fact that I was different in the period after the death, and so she looked extra carefully at me in an attempt to interpret me. Our pets do not attempt to comfort us, for the simple reason they do not understand that we need comfort, yet they can be such a great comfort during our most difficult times.

In Ecclesiastes (3:19), it says:

For what happens to the children of man and what happens to the beasts is the same; as one dies, so dies the other. They all have the same breath, and man has no advantage over the beasts.

We will all die, humans as well as animals. Some animals live for a very long time, for example clams can live to be four to five hundred years old. There are also jellyfish that can live forever, although in practice they get damaged or eaten, so there's no eternal life for them either. The Greenland shark has an estimated lifespan of two hundred years, and some studies have estimated that its maximum life expectancy could be over five hundred years. The bowhead whale also seems to be able to live for two hundred years. At the other end of the scale we find chameleons and house mice, which can last for a year provided they don't get injured or eaten; and not to mention mayflies, of which there are over 3,000 species, that live from a few hours to a few days. Average human life expectancy is increasing, but this varies from place to place. There are countries where it is as low as forty years, and other countries where it is twice that. Nevertheless, we have to say that there is nothing about our lifespan that makes us stand out. What is special about us is that we go through life conscious that life – both our own and others' – will end.

SIXTEEN

Do Animals Have Morals?

Animals can make decisions that seem to be moral. More than fifty years ago, researchers showed that rhesus monkeys refuse to accept food if it means that another monkey will receive a painful electric shock.[1] The monkeys could pull on a chain to get food, but they refused to do it if it meant that a fellow monkey received a shock. One monkey kept this going for twelve days without food. The same result is found in experiments with rats.[2] This seems to indicate that monkeys and rats – and other species that behave similarly – should be included in our ethics, not only as moral objects, but as moral subjects. However, that would probably not be to their benefit. When looked at through our moral spectacles, animals are, to a large extent, simply terrible creatures! Chimpanzees are among the worst. Their widespread practice of killing the offspring of other chimpanzees, and then eating them afterwards – something that both male and female chimpanzees do – is impossible to accept if you do not see this behaviour as outside of the moral realm. To the extent that animals are regarded as legitimate subjects for moral praise, they should also be considered legitimate subjects for moral blame. However, this can lead to quite absurd situations, as in the Middle Ages and especially during the Renaissance, when animals were put on trial.[3] One of the most famous examples of this concerns a French pig that in 1457 was charged with the premeditated murder of a five-year-old boy. Her six piglets were also charged and so the pig family were appointed their own defence lawyer to state their case. The sow was sentenced to death, but the piglets were acquitted considering their young age and because the mother had been such a poor influence on them. The reason we find trials like this so absurd is because we are drawing these animals into a normative universe in which they simply do not belong. The sow had no prerequisites for knowing that it is morally wrong to kill a boy. She had no prerequisites for being able to orientate herself within such a normative universe. So it becomes absurd to then treat her as if she did. But you could say, what about rats and rhesus monkeys? Did they not realize they were orientating themselves in a normative universe when they refused food because a fellow rat or rhesus monkey would get a shock? Not necessarily. It is quite conceivable that they were not aware of the pain their fellow species member was in, but that instead it was their unpleasant cries of pain that ruined their appetites. It would also have been concern for their own well-being and discomfort which motivated them. It is as the philosopher Thomas Hobbes once said when asked why he had given money to a beggar since he believed that all human actions were selfishly motivated: he was trying to relieve his own discomfort at seeing another person in need.

This can seem like a slightly uncharitable interpretation of animals, that we dismiss their ability to act morally because there are only slim grounds for it. However, there is some evidence of this being the case. In experiments on rats – where none of their companions received shocks but where pressing a lever to get food also triggered white noise – even fewer rats pressed the lever.[4]

You cannot just brush aside all the examples of helpful behaviour from animals that save other animals or humans, or of mothers of one species who show compassion for youngsters of another species. There are so many documented cases that it can no longer be dismissed as 'anecdotal'. Anecdotes of this magnitude are *data*. Nature isn't just red in tooth and claw, but also empathy and helpfulness. However, this ability to show empathy and helpfulness is not enough to justify calling it a moral being. A being can act morally only if (1) There are several action alternatives; (2) The being can *evaluate* these alternatives in a normative perspective; and (3) The being can *choose* between these alternatives. As far as we know, only humans are able to do this. This was, by the way, something Darwin agreed with. He wrote: 'A moral being is one who is capable of reflecting on his past actions and their motives – of approving of some and disapproving of others.'[5] He believed that only humans have this ability, but that other animals will eventually develop it.

This is why we can place moral demands on humans, but not on animals. It is why chimpanzees are *not* evil, even if their behaviour appears to be so when viewed through our moral spectacles. Man is the only creature that can *act* based upon *reasons*. This requires special cognitive abilities that other animals don't seem to have. Frans de Waal concludes that animals, his chimpanzees included, cannot *act* based upon *reasons*, and therefore do not have morals in the fullest sense; although he argues convincingly that they possess a range of characteristics that can be considered as building blocks on the road to morality.[6] It is, by the way, strange that it is more popular to compare humans with chimpanzees than to compare them with bonobos (pygmy chimpanzees), since we are just as closely related to bonobos. Where chimpanzee life is aggressive and arranged into a strict hierarchical system with the alpha male at the top, bonobo life is characterized by a flatter structure where females lead, there is very little rivalry among males over winning female favour, there is very little fighting, and everyone is constantly having sex. Bonobos are the hippies of the animal world. While killing others' offspring is common with chimpanzees, it has not been documented in bonobos. Of course, human life differs significantly from bonobo life, but it is just as similar as it is to chimpanzee life.

David Hume claims that animals possess certain natural virtues, such as courage, stamina, faithfulness and kindness, but he emphasizes that they lack the sense to recognize what virtues and vices are.[7] However, by ascribing natural virtues to them, he moves some way towards acknowledging a moral dimension to their lives. Can animals act out of a sense of sympathy for another animal or human being? It doesn't seem at all unreasonable. Within a biological explanatory framework, this behaviour would ultimately be seen as all about self-interest – either by passing on their own genes, through kin selection, or by expecting a corresponding favour in return. In any case, animals can be so emotionally equipped that they have a desire to help or alleviate the pain of others. To be emotionally tuned in a way that we would normally consider morally good. In that case, we can say that although animals shouldn't be regarded as moral entities, they may have a proto-moral behaviour. Some animals can draw distinctions similar to the moral distinctions we draw. Some chimpanzees distinguish between those who don't *want* to give them food and those who *cannot* give them food. In other words, they can assess a situation where the outcome is not consistent with their preferences based on a more sophisticated than exclusive view of what gives them a desired result.

A few animals exist just outside the door to the moral universe. But in order to cross the threshold, a number of mental qualities – which we have no reason to attribute to any animals – are required. Even though animals should not be credited with morals, if by 'moral' we mean something more than an ability to act on the basis of empathy, it does not mean that animals do not have moral status. The question is, then, what moral status should they have?

In an essay from 1975, the French philosopher Emmanuel Levinas writes about the dog Bobby.[8] One day Bobby wandered into the prison camp where Levinas and his Jewish fellow prisoners had become used to subhuman treatment from the guards. That they resembled and had the same behaviour as other people was irrelevant. They were *Jews*, and therefore had no place in humanity. Bobby, on the other hand, did not distinguish between

Jews and non-Jews, or 'subhumans' and humans. Instead, he greeted the Jewish prisoners with bright eyes and a wagging tail during the weeks he spent with them, before the guards chased him away. Bobby was not in the slightest doubt that Levinas and his fellow prisoners were humans, and acknowledged them in a way that the guards did not. In a sense, this dog was more of a human to Levinas than the prisoners' guards were; he refers to Bobby as 'the last Kantian in Nazi Germany', and not without irony, since Adolf Eichmann is known to have referred to himself as an admirer of Kant. From there, Levinas's essay takes a surprising turn for such a heartwarming story of this encounter between animal and human. He draws a clear distinction between humans and animals and aligns himself closely with Kant. Levinas underscores that Bobby did not have the 'brain capacity' required to universalize moral maxims, as Kant's ethics require.

In his *Anthropology*, Kant writes that man is 'a being altogether different in rank and dignity from things, such as irrational animals, with which one may deal and dispose at one's discretion'.[9] It should be added that, although Kant claims that animals should be considered as mere things, they are clearly not *quite* like other things. In his lectures on ethics, he claims that a man who shoots his dog when it is no longer of any use to him is acting wrongly.[10] But he wouldn't say that someone who throws away a pair of worn-out shoes was doing something wrong. Why does Kant think it would be wrong to shoot the dog? He denies that it would be an infringement of the dog's rights, because it has no rights. We also have no direct obligations towards the dog, but he believes we have some form of indirect obligations that are actually our obligations to ourselves. By treating animals inhumanely, we destroy our own humanity. We should therefore treat animals well because it furthers our ability to treat humans well. This only makes sense if the animal is a type of thing that is not quite like other things. Most people immediately think that a person who inflicts pain on an animal for his own pleasure is doing something wrong to the animal itself, and not just against his own moral personality. Levinas seems to be committed to such a Kantian view of an animal's moral status.

Bobby saw Levinas's face, but Levinas was unable to see Bobby's. It is extraordinary. For Levinas, the guards who didn't recognize him as a human being were within the ethical limits, as vulnerable beings with a need for protection; while Bobby, who actually acknowledged Levinas as a human, would not be protected by his ethics in the same way. Why should an inability to universalize maxims be so crucial for Levinas? He wouldn't have made the same conclusion about young children who have not yet acquired the ability to universalize maxims. The basic premise of Levinas's ethics is that the ethical springs from a face-to-face encounter with another person. The vulnerability that appears in this face is the source of morality's demands. So the question is: can only humans have a face? Can only humans accommodate ethics? It seems immediately obvious that Bobby had a face: he had two eyes, two ears, a nose and a mouth. Furthermore, there was an awareness attached to this face. It is apparent from Levinas's description of how Bobby recognized him and the other Jews as worthy human beings: you cannot be recognized by something that has no consciousness. What was it Bobby really lacked? Were his eyes the wrong colour or was his nose too long? To direct questions, Levinas answers that one cannot totally deny that an animal has a face, and claim, for example, that it is through its face that one understands a dog.[11]

Levinas understands that animals have needs, even though he believes that human needs are less clear-cut than an animal's because they are always interpreted culturally. However, it must then be said that even though an animal's needs are more clear-cut than a human's, they are just as essential, and in that lies a vulnerability. But an animal's face is not presented in the same 'pure form' that a human's is. Animal life, as Levinas sees it, is a life totally devoted to struggling for existence. It is a life beyond ethics, and the very reason that animals don't confront us with the same ethical power. He believes that animals have no ability to be genuinely interested in others, to care about another purely for the other's benefit.[12] Animal life is 'pure vitality' and the animal is 'trapped' by its needs. It lives its life absolutely enclosed by itself. Humanity, on the other hand, is characterized by an openness to others. Humans can transcend their biology, and that implies being able to sacrifice one's own life for another.

One might wonder about these statements. What Levinas and the other prisoners saw in Bobby's eyes cannot be described in any reasonable manner as 'a struggle for existence'. It was much more of a look of kindness and devotion. So absolute that it could be characterized as a look of openness. Levinas writes explicitly that Bobby 'welcomed' them. And what about animals that risk their lives for their own offspring or for their owners? More importantly: for an ethic that puts the vulnerability of others first, one would think that recognition of the vulnerability we actually share with animals is enough to incorporate them in the ethics – as Levinas understands ethics. He says, a little half-heartedly, that we should not allow animals to suffer unnecessarily because they undoubtedly can suffer, but leaves it at that.

SEVENTEEN

Humans and Other Animals

What do I really mean by the term 'animals'? In modern biology it is normal to define an animal as a multicellular organism, not capable of photosynthesis, which receives nutrition and digests it in an intestine. Which in that case means amoebas are not animals. There will also be creatures in a grey area, like sponges. Sponges have no organs or intestines, but they have different cells that perform various tasks, so in that respect they resemble animals. It is usual to include sponges with animals even though they lack several of the basic qualities required for something to be considered an animal. Nevertheless, it is clear that there is no unproblematic demarcation between animals and plants. When the 'animals' category is so colossal, and includes creatures with such extremely varied characteristics, it can be misleading to refer to them as if they were somehow uniform; as when we talk about what we mean by 'understanding animals'.

Most will understand 'animals' to be 'all animals other than humans'. The question is whether that is a suitable way to divide the world. It classifies the world so that man literally becomes unique, a being all to himself, while all other life with an ability for self-motion is grouped into something uniform. Just because we usually divide the world into humans on one side and animals on the other, it's easy to forget that humans are animals too. Darwin was certainly not the first to duly place us within the animal kingdom. For example, in a letter Linnaeus (Carl von Linné) writes saying that he cannot, based on natural history, find one generic difference between humans and monkeys. He continues that he would have been in trouble with the Church if he had called a man a monkey or a monkey a man, but emphasized that, as a natural scientist, he should have done just that.[1] However, we humans are strange animals with a few important qualities not found anywhere else in the animal kingdom; at least not to the same extent.

We have accepted Linnaeus' classification of animal life, which has been modified since his day, but we could also have used totally different classifications. Before Linnaeus, it was normal to classify animals based on how they moved (if they crawl, walk, swim or fly), where they spent their time (in the water, earth or air) or their shape. Such divisions have a degree of plausibility, and I have to admit that I have never quite come to terms with the fact that a whale is not a fish. Is the Australian platypus a reptile or a mammal? It depends on what you want to place emphasis on. The simplest answer is perhaps to say that the platypus is both a reptile and a mammal. The problem arises because we attempt to classify the world in a logical way, where an animal belongs in one category *or* the other. For the platypus itself, this is probably not such a big problem. Classifications will always have a degree of arbitrariness about them. We can classify the world in different ways, and then choose some of them even though we could have chosen to do it differently. There is something arbitrary about our classifications, and also our classification of the world as consisting of the animal kingdom on one side and us humans on the other. An important trait of these classifications is that they are also instrumental in how we experience the world. By dividing the world in such a way that all other animals are fundamentally different from us, we will also see them as being fundamentally different, to a larger extent.

Ultimately, separate individuals are all that exists. There are great variations between different individuals of the same species or race. Some dogs are brave, others are timid; some are social while others are shy; some are stable whereas others are volatile; and some are dominant while others are submissive. The same goes for cats. Even though my cats, Lasse and Geir, were twins with the same genes – and as a result were almost identical in appearance except that Lasse was considerably larger than Geir – and had spent every single day together, they had different personalities. General terms like 'cat' obscure these differences. To get a grip on the world, to get an overview of all these separate individuals, we must however use generalizations; and some generalizations will be more appropriate than others.

Among the accounts of what distinguishes humans from other animals, there have been many suggestions: having a soul, being self-aware, having an awareness of one's own mortality, having language, having comprehension, using tools, making tools, having a sense of humour, an awareness of history, an aesthetic sense, an ability to recognize an objective reality, an ability to think about thinking, morals and so on. In the past I believed that animals couldn't feel bored, and aligned myself with Johann Wolfgang von Goethe's assertion that monkeys would have been regarded as humans had they been able to become bored.[2] Now, I believe that monkeys can become bored, and the same goes for many other species – not that I will recognize them as human beings for that reason. The dividing line isn't *there*, but it's also notoriously difficult to say where it is.

More recently, it has been shown that an increasing number of the qualities once thought to be unique to humans are in fact present in related variants of many other animal species. Often, the characteristic is first established in monkeys, and then in other mammals, and in a few cases also in birds and other species. It's about characteristics like using tools, creating tools, communicating with signs, teaching, anticipating future events and so on. The use of tools is widespread. Egyptian vultures use rocks to crack open hard ostrich eggs, and sea otters use rocks to open clams. Chimpanzees use two rocks, almost like a hammer and anvil, to crush nuts.

Darwin claimed that *making* tools was unique to humans, but that doesn't add up either. In 1960, when Jane Goodall documented that chimpanzees in Tanzania not only used tools, but *made* them, it was a sensation. This was later confirmed by countless other studies. When making tools, they don't just keep trying blindly until they find a working solution to a practical problem. They will often ponder for a while before trying a particular solution. Chimpanzees crush leaves to make sponges which they can use to collect water from hollow tree trunks. They strip branches of leaves so they can be poked into small holes to collect insects. Even more impressive is that they combine different tools, so that they can use one to bore through a surface, another to expand the hole, and a third to collect the food inside. Adult chimpanzees teach their young how these tools are to be used, and they also seem to plan what tools are to be used in future by obtaining tools that are then stored until they are needed.

When it comes to countless characteristics, the distance between animals and humans is smaller than was previously thought. From that perspective we have good reason to argue that the difference between 'us' and 'them' has become smaller. On the other hand, many of the same studies have revealed the gap between how these abilities have emerged in other animals and how they have emerged in humans. To answer the question of what the crucial difference between humans and animals should be, we presumably have to answer the question that, according to Kant, addresses all other philosophical questions: what is man?

Is there anything at all that is uniquely human? One strong candidate is that we blush. Darwin described this as 'the most peculiar and the most human of all expressions.'[3] In a trivial sense, humans are of course unique. No other animal is quite like us. But in the same trivial sense, all other species are unique. Nor is any other animal like a cat. The question is more precisely whether we are unique in a non-trivial sense. One non-trivial difference is man's ability to take moral action and responsibility. Another answer is that our linguistic abilities make us unique. Which means we are then back at the Aristotelian definition of man as 'life that possesses language'.[4] Linguistic capability is a non-trivial difference, but a lack of language does not imply a lack of consciousness, thinking and emotion.

As David Hume saw it, humans differ from other animals not least because our lives are totally dependent on tools and the like.[5] Our more developed intellect is necessary for our survival because nature has equipped us so badly physically. We are so vulnerable that we need to make tools, build cabins and houses, weave clothes and so on, so that we don't succumb to the cruelty of nature. So one can contend that here Hume is putting the cart before the horse. It is the invention and development of different technologies which made the development of our intellect possible, and at the same time caused a decline in the natural characteristics required for survival without such an intellect. Perhaps we shouldn't even say that we invented technology but, on the contrary, it was technology that invented us. Humans can exist as the kind of creatures we are precisely because of technology. Technology existed before humans did, at least humans as they are today, and technology exists outside the human world too, such as the tools chimpanzees use. When our ancestors began striking stones together to make one sharp stone, they were not yet human. The development of technology was slower then than it is today, and it took an estimated 1 million years before anyone attached this sharp stone to a stick and made the first axe. Technology developments like this enabled the development of our larger brain, because it freed up resources.

It might seem obvious that you and I have far more in common with animals like chimpanzees, and dogs and cats, than any of these animals have with earthworms, for example. A division of the world in which we humans are on one side of the divide, and chimpanzees and earthworms are on the other, becomes lopsided. On the other hand, we should not under-estimate the huge difference between us and even our closest relatives among other species. As the American primatologist Marc Hauser has argued, in the end we will probably find that the difference between human and animal cognition, even a chim-panzee's, is greater than the difference between a chimpanzee and a beetle.[6] It is a strong assertion, and it is anything but clear how one should perform such a comparison, but it is equally clear that the difference is huge. If visitors came from another planet and tried to make an overview of all life on Earth, they wouldn't nec-essarily be making a grave mistake if they drew a clear distinction between humans and all other animals, so that humans formed one category and all other animals were placed in a separate one.

Without ignoring the huge differences between chimpan-zees, sparrows, salmon and worms, it's equally true that none of them have ever written a novel, discovered natural laws, made a computer or detonated an atomic bomb. None of them have ever considered the possibility of doing any of these things. No other species shows as much variation in customs and practices as humans do. My dog has a variety of strange behaviour patterns, and until I had seen many other whippets I thought that this was something peculiar to her, but exactly the same behavioural traits can be found in most other whippets. Whippets differ from poodles and German shepherds, and most whippets are rather similar.

The fairly fixed differences in behaviour between different breeds must be due to the genetic variation between them. After all, my dog's mannerisms aren't *so* flexible. There are variations between individuals, groups and breeds, and also between animals of the same species. For example, there are customs that can only be seen in chimpanzees in one area, and not in another, without there being any genetic variation to explain this difference; and we can claim that some species have what we can call a culture, but we are still nowhere near the cultural and individual variation we find among humans.

What about those animals closest to us biologically? Generally speaking, adult monkeys function at about the same level as a two- to three-year-old human child when tested for memory, using tools, and for their understanding of the relationship between cause and effect; and that is impressive, but far below the level that adult humans master. When we look at social skills, young children also perform far better than adult chimpanzees, and the children are totally superior when it comes to understanding another's gestures and intentions. Humans have an ability to learn from others, and not least to teach and communicate with each other, which surpasses everything we find in other animal species. Children as young as three or four years old realize that other people can have false beliefs: for example, they might think that something is in a box while the child itself knows that the box is empty. Chimpanzees never seem to learn this. Even though it is impressive when chimpanzees perform at the same level as a human two-year-old, it is worth remembering that the child at this point has just started its learning process, while the chimpanzee has reached its limit.

That we share 98 or 99 per cent of our genes with chimpanzees does not mean that 'humans are 99 per cent chimpanzee.' First, one can take this percentage with a pinch of salt. The percentage you end up with depends entirely on how you count. Normal estimates lie between 94 and 99 per cent, but I have seen estimates as low as 75 per cent. Based on one method of counting – which shows that we have about 98.5 per cent of our DNA in common with chimpanzees – 92 per cent of our DNA is also in common with mice, and 60 per cent with fruit flies. We share about 50 per cent of our DNA with bananas. We should no more say that a person is 'half banana', because the person concerned shares 50 per cent of his DNA with a banana, than we should say that he is 98.5 per cent chimpanzee. These percentages can't tell us that much, basically, because comparisons between organisms cannot be reduced to comparisons of their DNA. Humans are simply not monkeys, and that applies equally to genetics, anatomy and psychology. Monkeys are made to climb trees while humans are made to walk on the ground. Admittedly, monkeys can also walk on the ground, and humans can climb trees, but that's not where our strength lies.

Human cooperation is pretty unique. Just think of all the people who need to cooperate so that someone can read a book.

The author is, of course, important, but there is also the editor and the cover designer. Furthermore, paper has to be produced and shipped to a printers, where the text is applied to the paper and the pages are bound into a cover. Still more people provide distribution to bookstores and to readers. Before that, it was crucial for someone to make a pen, and just the amount of cooperation required to make something as easy as a pen, and get it into an author's hand, is quite startling. After that, someone had to make a computer and a text-editing program that the handwritten text could be typed into. The total amount of cooperation needed for a reader to be able to hold a book in his or her hand is simply enormous. No other animal species can cooperate with such complexity and make products using so many different procedures. There are millions of species in the world, and many of them build things like nests, anthills or dams, and many of them can, as we have seen, use or even make tools. Many species display an amazing and fascinating level of intelligence, but the distinction between we humans and everything else is considerable. Humanity is characterized by a variety of behaviours that surpass what we find in other species. Variations in behaviour found in other species can be explained mostly by genetic variation, but not always, since different behaviours are also found in groups living in separate places where there is very little genetic variation between the groups. We can talk about how certain traditions are passed on culturally by animals from generation to generation, but again it must be emphasized that this doesn't come close to the complexity we find in humans. There is overall very little genetic variation between humans, while the variation in behaviour is extremely high. We are flexible creatures.

Hume was concerned with how great the similarities between humans and other animals are, all in all, but he wasn't blind to the differences. Perhaps the most important difference is that animals have no ability for so-called 'metacognition', even if Hume didn't use that exact phrase. The point is that even though animals can *have* different mental states, they cannot *reflect* on these states. Your dog may feel dejected and it can also perceive that you feel dejected, but it cannot make its or your dejectedness into an object for reflection. As a human, you have an ability to understand both yourself and your dog, although it has to be acknowledged that your understanding of both will always be incomplete, but strictly speaking your dog can understand neither you nor itself.

If you're sat dejected at the bar, staring deep into your glass, and say 'My wife doesn't understand me,' then the answer would probably be that she actually does, even if it's not as well as she thinks, but better than practically everybody else. On the other hand, if you had stared equally deep into your glass and said, 'My dog doesn't understand me,' you would have slightly more weight behind your claim. But your dog can take part in what you are feeling, and that in itself is a form of understanding.

We humans are alone in being human. But we are not alone in being able to like, suffer, starve, be disgusted, long for something and love. There lies significant potential for community.

EIGHTEEN

Friendship

The French philosopher Jacques Derrida recounted in a lecture he gave how one morning he was watched by his cat while standing naked in the bathroom, and it surprised him that the animal's staring caused him to feel embarrassed.[1] I would think that few others, when being stared at by their cat or dog in the bathroom, would react like that. But, nonetheless, I think he has a point of further validity: that animals can see us, they can look back at us and address us, perhaps even look at us accusingly and thereby make us feel shame. When we encounter this stare that addresses us, the animals are not just a 'them', they also belong among 'us'.

Can one be friends with an animal? It depends on what one applies to the phrase 'friendship'. Aristotle claims that in all forms of friendship there is a mutual and obvious kindness, and those who are friends wish one another well.[2] He distinguishes between three forms of friendship. Friendships of utility are defined through the benefits gained from each other. There is also a friendship based on pleasure, where the other's company is comfortable and you can, for example, have fun together. The highest form of friendship, however, is a friendship of virtue among equals who wish each other well and admire each other's virtue. Kant describes friendship as the highest form of mutual love.[3] He also distinguishes between different types, which partly coincide with Aristotle's divisions. There are friendships of need and friendships of taste, and these are related to the Aristotelian friendships of utility and pleasure. In addition, Kant emphasizes a form of friendship consisting of the complete trust two people have in revealing thoughts, secrets and feelings for each other.[4] Neither Aristotle nor Kant would have been willing to consider the relationship between a human and an animal as a friendship relationship, and in both cases it would have been the animal's lack of language and reason that impeded the relationship. But I'm not convinced they're right about that. A lack of language and reason is incompatible with the ideal friendships Aristotle and Kant describe because they consist of an exchange between friends which is fundamentally linguistic. Without language, you cannot exchange thoughts about moral virtues or share secrets. It is not clear if the same is true of the other forms of friendship, utility and pleasure. Your relationship with an animal goes beyond purely satisfying your own emotional needs – there is also an element of care there that stems from an understanding of the animal's needs and a desire for the animal to live a good life.

When your cat is lying on your lap and it stretches out and then curls into a ball while purring, with its claws extending and retracting, it is clear that it likes its situation; and when the cat repeatedly tries to get into precisely your lap, it is more than reasonable to consider it as an expression that it likes you or loves you.

Some would say that you never really know what is going on in an animal's consciousness, and since animals lack language, there is so much that cannot be shared between humans and animals. That is true. However, there is also a great deal that cannot be shared between humans, and you can never be certain of what is happening in another person's consciousness. Even when you share an experience with close friends or someone you love, there are parts of this experience that are yours only, ones which you will never be able to fully convey. If you feel sad, you can convey to others *that* you are sad, but you will never be able to fully communicate just *how* this sadness feels. A dog will be able to detect a sadness that most people would miss completely. It doesn't think about your sadness but reacts to it, so you could say that it shares this sadness. The same applies when you are happy. But a human friend can be happy or sad on your behalf, which is something a dog or a cat can never do.

Although there are major differences between humans and other animals, the border between animal life and human life can be quite fluid. Animal life is not closed to us. Learning to understand animals is also learning to understand oneself. At least, to understand important aspects of oneself. Understanding is not just about learning to see the animal side of yourself, but also about learning to see the human side of the animal. My relationship with the dogs and cats I have lived with is not an inadequate or inferior version of the relationship I have, and have had, with other humans. The relationships are *different* for the simple reason that these animals are different from humans.

I am certain that I can have feelings that dogs and cats cannot have, such as feelings of shame or envy. On the other hand, I consider it more than likely that they have feelings that I do not have; and since I don't have these feelings, I cannot identify them in animals either; they will always remain unknown to me. Nevertheless, it is clear that there are large overlaps between our emotional lives, and it is in this dimension especially that we can *understand* animals, not just explain them.

The more you get to know a species, the more you begin to regard the separate members of that species as individuals – nobody is totally alike. This is particularly striking when it comes to animals that have a highly developed consciousness, where we can detect an element of individuality or a personality, if you will. There is *someone* there, and this *someone* differs from everyone else.

By living with an animal and developing a form of communication – where the animal learns to understand you, and you understand the animal – a common world is built. There will always be large parts of your world in which the animal cannot participate, and vice versa, but by living together the shared world becomes bigger.

This book is dedicated to my mother, who had an unusually good rapport with animals and who taught me to understand them when I was a child. What was it she taught me? She taught me to wait and not impose myself, but to let the animal introduce itself to me. She taught me to *listen* to the animal, and not least she taught me to *see* the animal. She taught me to allow the animal to tell me who it is through its behaviour. She taught me to have a calm openness towards animals, and if you have that, an understanding of the animal will emerge.

References

Introduction

1 Stephen Jay Gould, *Leonardo's Mountain of Clams and the Diet of Worms: Essays on Natural History* (Cambridge, MA, 1998), p. 376.
2 Martin Heidegger, *Prolegomena zur Geschichte des Zeitbegriffs* (Frankfurt am Main, 1988), pp. 409f.
3 Ludwig Wittgenstein, *Culture and Value*, trans. Peter Winch (Oxford, 1998), p. 24.

1 Wittgenstein's Lion and Kafka's Ape

1 Cf. Wittgenstein, *Philosophical Investigations*, trans. G.E.M. Anscombe (Oxford, 1986), p. 223.
2 For a good account of these signs, see Genevieve von Petzinger, *The First Signs: Unlocking the Mysteries of the World's Oldest Symbols* (New York and London, 2016).
3 Cf. Wittgenstein, *Philosophical Investigations*, § 206.
4 Ibid., p. 223.
5 Franz Kafka, 'A Report to an Academy', in *The Metamorphosis and Other Stories*, trans. Willa and Edwin Muir (New York, 1995).
6 Immanuel Kant, *Anthropology from a Pragmatic Point of View*, trans. Robert B. Louden (Cambridge, 2006), p. 233n.
7 Julien Offray de La Mettrie, *Machine Man and Other Writings*, trans. Ann Thomson (Cambridge and New York, 1996), pp. 11f.

2 Language

1 For a good, summarized overview and discussion around the research into the language of apes, see John Dupré, 'Conversations with Apes', in *Humans and Other Animals* (Oxford, 2006), chap. 11.
2 Cf. Kevin N. Laland, *Darwin's Unfinished Symphony: How Culture*

Made the Human Mind (Princeton, NJ, and Oxford, 2017), p. 178.

3 Marc D. Hauser, Noam Chomsky and W. T. Fitch, 'The Faculty of Language: What Is It, Who Has It, and How Did It Evolve?', *Science*, 298 (2002).

4 Cf. Ernst Cassirer, *An Essay on Man: An Introduction to a Philosophy of Human Culture* (New Haven, CT, 1944).

5 Ludwig Wittgenstein, *Philosophical Occasions, 1912–1951* (Indianapolis, IN, and Cambridge, 1993), p. 394.

6 Wittgenstein, *Philosophical Investigations*, trans. G.E.M. Anscombe (Oxford, 1986), § 206.

7 Wittgenstein, *Zettel, Werkausgabe*, vol. VIII (Frankfurt am Main, 1984), § 567.

3 Seeing Animal Consciousness

1 Ludwig Wittgenstein, *Philosophical Investigations*, trans. G.E.M. Anscombe (Oxford, 1986), p. 178.

2 Ibid., § 357.

3 Cf. ibid., p. 223.

4 Ibid., p. 213.

5 David Hume, *A Treatise of Human Nature* (London, 1984), p. 316.

6 Wittgenstein, *Philosophical Investigations*, § 647.

7 Cf. ibid., § 580.

8 Wittgenstein, *Bemerkungen über die Philosophie der Psychologie II, Werkausgabe*, vol. VII (Frankfurt am Main, 1984), § 570. Cf. Wittgenstein, *Zettel, Werkausgabe*, vol. VIII (Frankfurt am Main, 1984), § 225.

9 Cf. Wittgenstein, *Philosophical Investigations*, § 303.

10 Maurice Merleau-Ponty, *Phenomenology of Perception*, trans. Colin Smith (London, 1962), p. 184.

11 Wittgenstein, *Zettel*, § 526.

12 Wittgenstein, *Bemerkungen über die Philosophie der Psychologie II*, § 328.

13 Wittgenstein, *Zettel*, § 520.

14 Gregory Berns, *What It's Like to Be a Dog: And Other Adventures in Animal Neuroscience* (New York, 2017).

15 Michael S. Gazzaniga, *Who's in Charge? Free Will and the Science of the Brain* (New York, 2011), p. 190.

16 Adam P. Steiner and A. David Redish, 'Behavioral and
    Neurophysiological Correlates of Regret in Rat Decision-making
    on a Neuroeconomic Task', *Nature Neuroscience*, 17 (2014).

4 A Human Form

1 Conwy Lloyd Morgan, *An Introduction to Comparative Psychology*
    (London, 1894), p. 53.
2 Conwy Lloyd Morgan, *Animal Life and Intelligence*
    (London, 1890–91), pp. 398f.
3 Frans B. M. de Waal, 'Anthropomorphism and Anthropodenial:
    Consistency in Our Thinking about Humans and Other Animals',
    Philosophical Topics, XXVII/1 (1999).
4 Zana Bahlig-Pieren and Dennis C. Turner, 'Anthropomorphic
    Interpretations and Ethological Descriptions of Dog and Cat
    Behavior by Lay People', *Anthrozoös*, XII/4 (1999).
5 David Hume, *A Treatise of Human Nature* (London, 1984),
    p. 226.
6 Daniel Dennett, 'True Believers', in *The Intentional Stance*
    (Cambridge, MA, 1987).

5 Mind-reading

1 Fritz Heider and Marianne Simmel, 'An Experimental Study of
    Apparent Behavior', *American Journal of Psychology*, LVII/2 (1944).
2 René Descartes, *The Philosophical Writings of Descartes*, vol. III:
    The Correspondence, trans. John Cottingham et al. (Cambridge, 1991),
    pp. 100, 203f.
3 Ibid., p. 99.
4 Descartes, *The Philosophical Writings of Descartes*, vol. I, trans.
    John Cottingham et al. (Cambridge, 1985), pp. 139ff.
5 Descartes, *The Correspondence*, p. 304.
6 Ibid., pp. 61f.
7 Ibid., pp. 148f.
8 Ibid., p. 365.
9 Peter Carruthers, 'Brute Experience', *Journal of Philosophy*, LXXXVI/5
    (1989).
10 Immanuel Kant, *Träume eines Geistersehers, erläutert durch Träume
    der Metaphysik*, in *Kants gesammelte Schriften*, vol. II (Berlin, 1902–),
    s. 324f.

11 Peter Godfrey-Smith, *Other Minds: The Octopus, the Sea, and the Deep Origins of Consciousness* (New York, 2016).
12 Ned Block, 'Consciousness', in *The Oxford Companion to the Mind*, ed. Richard L. Gregory, 2nd edn (Oxford, 2004).
13 Melvyn Goodale and David Milner, *Sight Unseen: An Exploration of Conscious and Unconscious Vision*, 2nd edn (Oxford, 2017).
14 For example, see Michael Tye, *Tense Bees and Shell-shocked Crabs: Are Animals Conscious?* (Oxford, 2017).

6 Intelligence

1 Cf. Adriana S. Benzaquén, *Encounters with Wild Children: Temptation and Disappointment in the Study of Human Nature* (Montreal and London, 2006).
2 Hans-Georg Gadamer, *Wahrheit und Methode. Grundzüge einer philosophischen Hermeneutik. Gesammelte Werke*, vol. 1 (Tübingen, 1990), p. 392.
3 Laasya Samhita and Hans J. Gross, 'The "Clever Hans Phenomenon" Revisited', *Communicative and Integrative Biology*, VI/6 (2013).
4 Cf. Carl Safina, *Beyond Words: What Animals Think and Feel* (New York, 2015), p. 203.
5 Cf. Clive D. L. Wynne and Monique A. R. Udell, *Animal Cognition: Evolution, Behavior and Cognition*, 2nd edn (London, 2013), p. 41.
6 Alex Thornton and Katherine McAuliffe, 'Teaching in Wild Meerkats', *Science*, 313 (2006).

7 For Now We See through a Mirror, Darkly

1 Immanuel Kant, *Logik*, in *Kants gesammelte Schriften*, vol. XVI (Berlin and New York, 1902–), *Reflexion*, 3444.
2 Alex Thornton and Dieter Lukas, 'Individual Variation in Cognitive Performance: Developmental and Evolutionary Perspectives', *Philosophical Transactions of the Royal Society B*, 367 (2012).
3 Ibid.
4 Clive D. L. Wynne and Monique A. R. Udell, *Animal Cognition: Evolution, Behavior and Cognition*, 2nd edn (London, 2013), p. 174.
5 Ibid., pp. 175f.
6 Kant, *Anthropology from a Pragmatic Point of View*, trans. Robert B. Louden (Cambridge, 2006), § 1.

7 Kant, *Kritik der Urteilskraft*, in *Kants gesammelte Schriften*, vol. v (Berlin and New York, 1902–), p. 464, *Anthropology*, p. 212.
8 Søren Kierkegaard, *Sygdommen til døden, Samlede Verker*, vol. xi, 2nd edn (Copenhagen, 1923), p. 143.

8 Time

1 Seneca, *Selected Philosophical Letters*, trans. Brad Inwood (Oxford and New York, 2007), p. 102.
2 Henri Bergson, *Matter and Memory*, trans. Nancy Morgan Paul and W. Scott Palmer (New York, 1991), pp. 82f.
3 Cf. Frans de Waal, *Are We Smart Enough to Know How Smart Animals Are?* (London, 2016), pp. 119f.
4 Mathias Osvath, 'Spontaneous Planning for Future Stone Throwing by a Male Chimpanzee', *Current Biology*, xix/5 (2009).
5 Michel Jouvet, 'Behavioural and eeg Effects of Paradoxical Sleep Deprivation in the Cat', *Excerpta Medica International Congress Series No. 87, Proceedings of the xxiiird International Congress of Physiological Sciences* [1960] (Tokyo, 1965).
6 Nicola S. Clayton and Anthony Dickinson, 'Episodic-like Memory during Cache Recovery by Scrub Jays', *Nature*, 395 (1998).
7 Homer, *The Odyssey*, trans. Emily Wilson (New York and London, 2017), book 17, 290–327.

9 Can Animals Be Understood?

1 Wilhelm Dilthey, *Der Aufbau der geschichtlichen Welt in den Geisteswissenschaften* (Frankfurt am Main, 1970).
2 Wilhelm Dilthey, *Grundlegung der Wissenschaften vom Menschen, der Gesellschaft und der Geschichte* (Göttingen, 1982), p. 345.
3 Hans-Georg Gadamer, *Wahrheit und Methode. Grundzüge einer philosophischen Hermeneutik. Gesammelte Werke*, vol. i (Tübingen, 1990), p. 457, cf. p. 447.
4 Martin Heidegger, *Die Grundbegriffe der Metaphysik. Welt – Endlichkeit – Einsamkeit* (Frankfurt am Main, 1992 [1929–30]), p. 409.
5 Ibid., § 42.
6 Ibid., pp. 384, 416.
7 Martin Heidegger, *Sein und Zeit* (Tübingen, 1986), p. 68.
8 Ibid., p. 161.

9 Martin Heidegger, *Prolegomena zur Geschichte des Zeitbegriffs* (Frankfurt am Main, 1988), p. 373.
10 Heidegger, *Sein und Zeit*, p. 157.
11 Donald Griffin, *Animal Minds* (Chicago, IL, 1992).
12 See Heidegger, *Einführung in die phänomenologische Forschung* (Frankfurt am Main, 1994), p. 22.
13 Martin Heidegger, *Wegmarken* (Frankfurt am Main, 1976), pp. 313, 333.
14 Martin Heidegger, *Heraklit* (Frankfurt am Main, 1979), p. 217.
15 Heidegger, *Sein und Zeit*, p. 141.
16 Martin Heidegger, *Nietzsche, Erster Band* (Pfullingen, 1989), p. 119.
17 Max Scheler, *Wesen und Formen der Sympathie*, 2nd edn (Bonn, 1923).

10 Surroundings

1 The presentation of Uexküll is mainly based on *Kompositionslehre der Natur. Biologie als undogmatische Naturwissenschaft* (Frankfurt am Main, Berlin and Vienna, 1980).
2 Michel de Montaigne, 'An Apology for Raymond Sebond', in *The Complete Essays*, trans. M. A. Screech (London, 2003).
3 Friedrich Nietzsche, *Philosophy and Truth: Selections from Nietzsche's Notebooks of the Early 1870s*, ed. and trans. Daniel Breazeale (London, 1990), p. 86.
4 Plato, *Theaetetus*, trans. M. J. Levett (Indianapolis, IN, and Cambridge, 1992), 152a.
5 Ibid., 161c.

11 To Be an Animal

1 Charles Foster, *Being a Beast* (London, 2016).
2 Thomas Nagel, 'What Is It Like to Be a Bat?', *Philosophical Review*, LXXXIII/4 (1974).
3 Jaak Panskepp, *Affective Neuroscience: The Foundations of Human and Animal Emotions* (Oxford, 1998).
4 Cf. Aaron Ben-Ze'ev, *The Subtlety of Emotions* (Cambridge, MA, and London, 2000).

12 The Dog

1 Mietje Germonpréa et al., 'Fossil Dogs and Wolves from Palaeolithic Sites in Belgium, the Ukraine and Russia: Osteometry, Ancient

DNA and Stable Isotopes', *Journal of Archaeological Science*, XXXVI/2 (2009).
2 Krista Macpherson and William A. Roberts, 'Do Dogs (*Canis familiaris*) Seek Help in an Emergency?', *Journal of Comparative Psychology*, CXX/2 (2006).

13 The Cat

1 Michel de Montaigne, 'An Apology for Raymond Sebond', in *The Complete Essays*, trans. M. A. Screech (London, 2003).
2 Jean-Denis Vigne et al., 'Early Taming of the Cat in Cyprus', *Science*, CCCIV/259 (2004).
3 Cf. Abigail Tucker, *The Lion in the Living Room* (New York, 2016).

14 The Octopus

1 The account of the octopus is particularly indebted to Peter Godfrey-Smith, *Other Minds: The Octopus, the Sea, and the Deep Origins of Consciousness* (New York, 2016). I've also learnt a great deal from Sy Montgomery, *The Soul of an Octopus: A Surprising Exploration into the Wonder of Consciousness* (New York, 2015).
2 Johan Huizinga, *Homo ludens* (London, 1980), p. 2.

15 Loneliness and Grief

1 Denise Aydinonat et al., 'Social Isolation Shortens Telomeres in African Grey Parrots (*Psittacus erithacus erithacus*)', *PLoS One*, IX/4 (2014).
2 Akiko Koto and Brian Hollis, 'Social Isolation Causes Mortality by Disrupting Energy Homeostasis in Ants', *Behavioral Ecology and Sociobiology*, LXIX/4 (2015).
3 Cf. Lars Svendsen, *A Philosophy of Loneliness*, trans. Kerri Pierce (London, 2017).
4 Cf. Barbara J. King, *How Animals Grieve* (Chicago, IL, 2013).
5 Frans de Waal, *The Bonobo and the Atheist: In Search of Humanism among the Primates* (New York, 2013), p. 210.
6 Sigmund Freud, 'Trauer und Melancholie', *Essays II* (Berlin, 1989), pp. 104f.
7 Jane Goodall, *Through a Window: My Thirty Years with the Chimpanzees of Gombe* (Boston, MA, 1990), p. 196.

16 Do Animals Have Morals?

1 Stanley Wechkin, J. H. Masserman and W. Terris, 'Shock to a Conspecific as an Aversive Stimulus', *Psychonomic Science*, 1 (1964).

2 Russell M. Church, 'Emotional Reactions of Rats to the Pain of Others', *Journal of Comparative and Physiological Psychology*, LII/2 (1959).

3 A comprehensive historical overview, containing numerous fascinating legal documents from these animal court trials, can be found in Edward Payson Evans's *The Criminal Prosecution and Capital Punishment of Animals* (London, 1906). A more recent account and discussion can be found in Jen Girgen's 'The Historical and Contemporary Prosecution and Punishment of Animals', *Animal Law*, XCVII (2003).

4 Jf. Marc Hauser, *Wild Minds: What Animals Really Think* (New York, 2000), p. 120.

5 Charles Darwin, *The Descent of Man and Selection in Relation to Sex*, vol. 1 (Princeton, NJ, 1981), s. 88f.

6 Frans de Waal, *Good Natured: The Origins of Right and Wrong in Humans and Other Animals* (Cambridge, MA, 1997), p. 209.

7 David Hume, *A Treatise of Human Nature*, book 3.1.1 (London, 1984).

8 Emmanuel Levinas, 'The Name of a Dog, or Natural Rights', in *Difficult Freedom: Essays on Judaism*, trans. Seán Hand (Baltimore, MD, 1997).

9 Immanuel Kant, *Anthropology from a Pragmatic Point of View*, trans. Robert B. Louden (Cambridge, 2006), § 1.

10 Kant, *Vorlesungen über Ethik*, in *Kants gesammelte Schriften*, vol. XXVII (Berlin/New York, 1902–), p. 212.

11 Robert Bernasconi and David Woods, eds, *The Provocation of Levinas: Rethinking the Other* (London and New York, 1998), p. 169.

12 Emmanuel Levinas, *Of God Who Comes to Mind*, trans. Bettina Bergo (Stanford, CA, 1998), pp. 152f.

17 Humans and Other Animals

1 Carl von Linné, letter to Johann Georg Gmelin, 25 February 1747, http://linnaeus.c18.net.

2 Johann Wolfgang von Goethe, *West-östlicher Divan, Epen. Maximen und Reflexionen, Goethes poetische Werke zweiter Band* (Stuttgart, 1950), s. 791.

3 Charles Darwin, *The Expression of the Emotions in Man and Animals* (Cambridge, 2009), chap. 13.
4 Aristotle, *Politics*, trans. E. Barker (Oxford, 2009), 1253a.
5 David Hume, *A Treatise of Human Nature* (London, 1984), p. 226.
6 Cf. Frans B. M. de Waal, *Are We Smart Enough to Know How Smart Animals Are?* (London, 2016), p. 121.

18 Friendship

1 Jacques Derrida, *The Animal That Therefore I Am*, trans. David Wills (New York, 2008).
2 Aristotle, *Nicomachean Ethics*, trans. T. Irwin (Indianapolis, IN, and Cambridge, 1999), 1156a9.
3 Immanuel Kant, *Vorlesungen über Ethik*, in *Kants gesammelte Schriften*, vol. XXVII (Berlin/New York, 1902–), p. 423.
4 Kant, *Metaphysik der Sitten*, in *Kants gesammelte Schriften*, vol. XI (Berlin and New York, 1902–), p. 471.

Bibliography

Aristotle, *Nicomachean Ethics*, trans. T. Irwin (Indianapolis, IN, and Cambridge, 1999)
——, *Politics*, trans. E. Barker (Oxford, 2009)
Aydinonat, Denise, et al., 'Social Isolation Shortens Telomeres in African Grey Parrots (Psittacus erithacus erithacus)', *PLoS One*, IX/4 (2014)
Bahlig-Pieren, Zana, and Dennis C. Turner, 'Anthropomorphic Interpretations and Ethological Descriptions of Dog and Cat Behavior by Lay People', *Anthrozoös*, XII (1999)
Benzaquén, Adriana S., *Encounters with Wild Children: Temptation and Disappointment in the Study of Human Nature* (Montreal and London, 2006)
Ben-Ze'ev, Aaron, *The Subtlety of Emotions* (Cambridge, MA, and London, 2000)
Bergson, Henri, *Matter and Memory*, trans. Nancy Morgan Paul and W. Scott Palmer (New York, 1991)
Bernasconi, Robert and David Woods, eds, *The Provocation of Levinas: Rethinking the Other* (London and New York, 1998)
Berns, Gregory, *What It's Like to Be a Dog: And Other Adventures in Animal Neuroscience* (New York, 2017)
Block, Ned, 'Consciousness', in *The Oxford Companion to the Mind*, ed. Richard L. Gregory, 2nd edn (Oxford, 2004)
Carruthers, Peter, 'Brute Experience', *Journal of Philosophy*, LXXXVI/5 (1989)
Cassirer, Ernst, *An Essay on Man: An Introduction to a Philosophy of Human Culture* (New Haven, CT, 1944)
Church, Russell M., 'Emotional Reactions of Rats to the Pain of Others', *Journal of Comparative and Physiological Psychology*, LII/2 (1959)
Clayton, Nicola S., and Anthony Dickinson, 'Episodic-like Memory during Cache Recovery by Scrub Jays', *Nature*, CCCXCV (1998)
Darwin, Charles, *The Descent of Man and Selection in Relation to Sex*, vol. I (Princeton, NJ, 1981)
——, *The Expression of the Emotions in Man and Animals* (Cambridge, 2009)

Dennett, Daniel, *The Intentional Stance* (Cambridge, MA, 1987)

Derrida, Jacques, *The Animal That Therefore I Am*, trans. David Wills (New York, 2008)

Descartes, René, *The Philosophical Writings of Descartes*, vol. I, trans. John Cottingham et al. (Cambridge, 1985)

——, *The Philosophical Writings of Descartes*, vol. III: *The Correspondence*, trans. John Cottingham et al. (Cambridge, 1991)

Dilthey, Wilhelm, *Der Aufbau der geschichtlichen Welt in den Geisteswissenschaften* (Suhrkamp, 1970)

——, *Grundlegung der Wissenschaften vom Menschen, der Gesellschaft und der Geschichte* (Göttingen, 1982)

Dupré, John, *Humans and Other Animals* (Oxford, 2006)

Evans, Edward Payson, *The Criminal Prosecution and Capital Punishment of Animals* (London, 1906)

Foster, Charles, *Being a Beast* (London 2016)

Freud, Sigmund, 'Trauer und Melancholie', *Essays II* (Berlin, 1989)

Gadamer, Hans-Georg, *Wahrheit und Methode. Grundzüge einer philosophischen Hermeneutik. Gesammelte Werke*, vol. I (Tübingen, 1990)

Gazzaniga, Michael S., *Who's in Charge? Free Will and the Science of the Brain* (New York, 2011)

Germonpréa, Mietje et al., 'Fossil Dogs and Wolves from Palaeolithic Sites in Belgium, the Ukraine and Russia: Osteometry, Ancient DNA and Stable Isotopes', *Journal of Archaeological Science*, XXXVI/2 (2009)

Girgen, Jen, 'The Historical and Contemporary Prosecution and Punishment of Animals', *Animal Law*, XCVII (2003)

Godfrey-Smith, Peter, *Other Minds: The Octopus, the Sea, and the Deep Origins of Consciousness* (New York, 2016)

Goethe, Johann Wolfgang von, *West-östlicher Divan, Epen. Maximen und Reflexionen, Goethes poetische Werke zweiter Band* (Stuttgart, 1950)

Goodale, Melvyn, and David Milner, *Sight Unseen: An Exploration of Conscious and Unconscious Vision*, 2nd edn (Oxford, 2017)

Goodall, Jane, *Through a Window: My Thirty Years with the Chimpanzees of Gombe* (Boston, MA, 1990)

Gould, Stephen Jay, *Leonardo's Mountain of Clams and the Diet of Worms: Essays on Natural History* (Cambridge, MA, 1998)

Griffin, Donald, *Animal Minds* (Chicago, IL, 1992)

Hauser, Marc, *Wild Minds: What Animals Really Think* (New York, 2000)

Hauser, Marc D., Noam Chomsky and W. T. Fitch, 'The Faculty
of Language: What is It, Who has It, and How Did it
Evolve', *Science*, CCXCVIII (2002)
Heidegger, Martin, *Wegmarken* (Frankfurt a.M., 1976)
——, *Heraklit* (Frankfurt a.m., 1979)
——, *Sein und Zeit* (Tübingen, 1986)
——, *Prolegomena zur Geschichte des Zeitbegriffs* (Frankfurt a.m., 1988)
——, *Nietzsche, Erster Band* (Pfullingen, 1989)
——, *Die Grundbegriffe der Metaphysik. Welt – Endlichkeit – Einsamkeit.*
(Frankfurt a.m., 1992)
——, *Einführung in die phänomenologische Forschung*
(Frankfurt a.m., 1994)
Heider, Fritz, and Marianne Simmel, 'An Experimental Study of Apparent
Behavior', *American Journal of Psychology*, LVII/2 (1944)
Homer, *The Odyssey*, trans. Emily Wilson (New York and London,
2017)
Huizinga, Johan, *Homo ludens* (London, 1980)
Hume, David, *A Treatise of Human Nature* (London, 1984)
Jouvet, Michel, 'Behavioural and EEG Effects of Paradoxical Sleep
Deprivation in the Cat', *Excerpta Medica International Congress Series
No. 87 Proceedings of the XXIIIrd International Congress of Physiological
Sciences* (Tokyo, 1965)
Kafka, Franz, 'A Report to an Academy', in *The Metamorphosis
and Other Stories*, trans. Willa and Edwin Muir (New York, 1995)
Kant, Immanuel, *Träume eines Geistersehers, erläutert durch Träume
der Metaphysik, Kants gesammelte Schriften*, vol. II
(Berlin, 1902)
——, *Metaphysik der Sitten, Kants gesammelte Schriften*, vol. VI
(Berlin and New York, 1902–)
——, *Kritik der Urteilskraft, Kants gesammelte Schriften Bd.* V
(Berlin and New York, 1902–)
——, *Logik, Kants gesammelte Schriften*, vol. XVI (Berlin
and New York, 1902)
——, *Vorlesungen über Ethik, Kants gesammelte Schriften*, vol. XXVII
(Berlin and New York, 1902–)
——, *Anthropology From a Pragmatic Point of View,* trans. Robert B.
Louden (Cambridge, 2006)
Kierkegaard, Søren, *Sygdommen til døden, Samlede Verker*, vol. XI,
2nd edn (København 1923)
King, Barbara J., *How Animals Grieve* (Chicago, IL, 2013)

Koto, Akiko and Brian Hollis, 'Social Isolation Causes Mortality by Disrupting Energy Homeostasis in Ants', *Behavioral Ecology and Sociobiology*, LXIX/4 (2015)

Laland, Kevin N., *Darwin's Unfinished Symphony: How Culture Made the Human Mind* (Princeton, NJ, and Oxford, 2017)

La Mettrie, Julien Offray de, *Machine Man and Other Writings*, trans. Ann Thomson (Cambridge and New York, 1996)

Levinas, Emmanuel, 'The Name of a Dog, or Natural Rights', in *Difficult Freedom: Essays on Judaism*, trans. Seán Hand (Baltimore, MD, 1997)

——, *Of God Who Comes to Mind*, trans. Bettina Bergo (Stanford, CA, 1998)

Macpherson, Krista, and William A. Roberts, 'Do Dogs (*Canis familiaris*) Seek Help in an Emergency?', *Journal of Comparative Psychology*, CXX/2 (2006)

Merleau-Ponty, Maurice, *Phenomenology of Perception*, trans. Colin Smith (London, 1962)

Montaigne, Michel de, 'An Apology for Raymond Sebond', *The Complete Essays*, trans M. A. Screech (London, 2003)

Montgomery, Sy, *The Soul of an Octopus: A Surprising Exploration into the Wonder of Consciousness* (New York, 2015)

Morgan, Conwy Lloyd, *Animal Life and Intelligence* (London, 1890–91)

——, *An Introduction to Comparative Psychology* (London, 1894)

Nagel, Thomas, 'What Is It Like to Be a Bat?', *Philosophical Review*, LXXXIII/4 (1974)

Nietzsche, Friedrich, *Philosophy and Truth: Selections from Nietzsche's Notebooks of the Early 1870s*, ed. and trans. Daniel Breazeale (London, 1990)

Osvath, Mathias, 'Spontaneous Planning for Future Stone Throwing by a Male Chimpanzee', *Current Biology*, XVIX/5 (2009)

Panskepp, Jaak, *Affective Neuroscience: The Foundations of Human and Animal Emotions* (Oxford, 1998)

Petzinger, Genevieve von, *The First Signs: Unlocking the Mysteries of the World's Oldest Symbols* (New York and London, 2016)

Plato, *Theaetetus*, trans M. J. Levett (Indianapolis, IN, and Cambridge, 1992)

Safina, Carl, *Beyond Words: What Animals Think and Feel* (New York, 2015)

Samhita, Laasya and Hans J. Gross, 'The "Clever Hans Phenomenon" Revisited', *Communicative and Integrative Biology*, VI/6 (2013)

Scheler, Max, *Wesen und Formen der Sympathie*, 2nd edn (Bonn, 1923)

Seneca, *Selected Philosophical Letters*, trans. Brad Inwood
(Oxford and New York, 2007)
Steiner, Adam P., and A. David Redish, 'Behavioral and
Neurophysiological Correlates of Regret in Rat Decision-making
on a Neuroeconomic Task', *Nature Neuroscience*, XVII (2014)
Svendsen, Lars, *A Philosophy of Loneliness*, trans Kerri Pierce
(London, 2017)
Thornton, Alex, and Dieter Lukas, 'Individual Variation in Cognitive
Performance: Developmental and Evolutionary Perspectives',
Philosophical Transactions of the Royal Society B, 367 (2012)
Thornton, Alex, and Katherine McAuliffe, 'Teaching in Wild Meerkats',
Science, XXXVIII (2006)
Tucker, Abigail, *The Lion in the Living Room* (New York, 2016)
Tye, Michael, *Tense Bees and Shell-shocked Crabs: Are Animals Conscious?*
(Oxford, 2017)
Uexküll, Jakob von, *Kompositionslehre der Natur: Biologie als
undogmatische Naturwissenschaft* (Frankfurt a.M., Berlin and Vienna,
1980)
Vigne, Jean-Denis et al., 'Early Taming of the Cat in Cyprus', *Science*,
CCCIV/259 (2004)
Waal, Frans B. M. De, 'Anthropomorphism and Anthropodenial:
Consistency in Our Thinking about Humans and Other Animals',
Philosophical Topics, XXVII/1 (1999)
——, *Good Natured: The Origins of Right and Wrong in Humans and Other
Animals* (Cambridge, MA, 1997)
——, *The Bonobo and the Atheist: In Search of Humanism among the
Primates* (New York, 2013)
——, *Are We Smart Enough to Know How Smart Animals Are?*
(London, 2016)
Wechkin, Stanley, J. H. Masserman and W. Terris, 'Shock to a Conspecific
as an Aversive Stimulus', *Psychonomic Science*, I (1964)
Wittgenstein, Ludwig, *Zettel, Werkausgabe, Bd. 8* (Frankfurt a.M., 1984)
——, *Bemerkungen über die Philosophie der Psychologie II, Werkausgabe*,
vol. VII (Frankfurt a.M., 1984)
——, *Philosophical Investigations*, trans. G.E.M. Anscombe (Oxford, 1986)
——, *Culture and Value*, trans. Peter Winch (Oxford, 1998)
——, *Philosophical Occasions, 1912–1951* (Indianapolis, IN, and Cambridge,
1993)
Wynne, Clive D. L., and Monique A. R. Udell, *Animal Cognition:
Evolution, Behavior and Cognition*, 2nd edn (London, 2013)

Acknowledgements

First of all, I would like to thank Fia, Fridtjof, Astor, Lasse, Geir and Luna – the animals I have lived with so far. Plus a huge thank you to Siri Sørlie and Iben Sørlie for their helpful suggestions, their enthusiasm, and for putting up with me while I have been so obsessed with my writing. I would also like to thank Joakim Botten, Erling Kagge, Erik Thorstensen, Espen Gamlund, Lene Renneflott and Dag Hessen for their helpful comments on my manuscript.